The Bible
and Its Wines

The Bible and Its Wines

by
Charles Wesley Ewing, D.D.

First Edition — First Printing

Published By:
The National Prohibition Foundation
Post Office Box 2635
Denver, Colorado 80201

Produced By:
Specialty Publishing, Inc.
1387 S. Inca Street
Denver, Colorado 80223

Library of Congress Cataloging in Publication Data

Ewing, Charles Wesley, 1912-
    The Bible and its wines.

    Bibliography: p.
    1. Wine—Biblical teaching. 2. Bible—Criticism,
interpretation, etc.   I. Title.
BS680.W55E84 1982   220.8′64122   85-14270
ISBN 1-737100-50-9

SPI/J/J 10 9 8 7 6 5 4 3 2 1

Dedicated to
HELEN MAE EWING

who has rejoiced with me in times of gladness; comforted me in sorrow, strengthened me in life's adversities; interceded for me when death's shadow hovered o'er; gave birth to our three children: Dwight David, Anna Mae and Sarah Lu; made our home a haven of rest and welcome to friend and stranger; made my ministry possible by her sacrificial labors; and deserves equal credit for whatever I have accomplished during the thirty-five years of our blest companionship.

Table of Contents

Preface

Frances Willard, great leader in both the Woman's Christian Temperance Union and the Prohibition Party often said "The liquor traffic would destroy the Church if it could but the Church could destroy the liquor traffic if it would."

Sixty years ago Bible-believing pastors, seminaries and Bible colleges as well as the members of sound churches were almost universally in agreement that the Bible, God's Holy Word teaches total abstinence from alcoholic beverages.

Today, many have departed from that position and many new pastors know virtually nothing regarding this subject because so few Christian educational institutions deal with it at all.

This fine book, the result of decades of study and research by Dr. Ewing, can be used of God to lead Christians back to a Biblical stance on the alcohol question.

I have had the privilege of knowing Dr. Charles Wesley Ewing for more than twenty-five years. His whole life and ministry have been marked by a deep love for the Lord and the people of the Lord.

Dr. Ewing currently pastors the Campbell Memorial United Methodist Church in Ferndale, Michigan and is President of the Evangelical Church Alliance, a ministerial association with more than 1,500 members.

His career has included many years of service to the temperance movement. He has been the Assistant Superintendent of the Illinois Temperance League in which capacity he led many successful local option battles. He has served as National Chairman of the Prohibition Party, Chairman of the Michigan Prohibition Party and on the Executive Committee of the National Temperance and Prohibition Council. He is now the Vice President of the National Prohibition Foundation, Inc.

When faced with a decision as to whether a practice or habit is right or wrong, the dedicated Christian asks "What saith the Lord?" Dr. Ewing has clearly given us the Biblical answer insofar as the use of alcoholic beverages is concerned. May we honestly face the facts and glorify our blessed Savior by obeying Him in this important matter and in all other areas of our walk.

— Earl F. Dodge Chairman,
National Prohibition Party
Denver, Colorado

Introduction

A re-examination of the subject of Bible wines is long overdue. In the last fifty years small pamphlets and tracts have appeared but none of them have been sufficient to meet all the questions that confront the average Bible student. During the nineteenth century numerous articles were published in magazines and in book form, both in America and in Britain, dealing with the Hebrew and Greek words rendered wine and strong drink in our English versions and showing how these words at times could not possibly refer to a fermented beverage. Unfortunately these works are no longer available. That there are questions that need answers is apparent to anyone who makes a mere cursory study of the Bible and wine.

All persons who read the Scriptures agree that wine was part of the common diet in Bible times. But here the agreement ends and two opposing positions are taken. On one side are those who maintain that Bible wine was always fermented. On the other side are those who declare that wine in Bible days was not always fermented, that the unfermented grape juice in its different forms is wine, that wine simply means the juice of the grape, and in many instances refers to the grape itself. Here the lines are drawn.

To resolve the issue, we must have a clear understanding of the meaning of meanings of Hebrew and Greek words translated wine. It actually becomes a matter of definition. However, in many instances a mere definition is not enough for some of the Hebrew and Greek words dealing with the subject, as well as our English word wine, are generic terms with multiple meanings, and to determine which meaning is intended the way the word is used in the particular scripture must be studied. It is a principle adhered to in legal proceedings that the meaning of a word at times is determined by its use in the sentence and also by the intent of the writer. This principle must be recognized in Biblical interpretation.

With this in mind, I have endeavored to determine the true meaning or meanings of Hebrew and Greek words dealing with wine and strong drink by consulting the works of Biblical language scholars, Hebrew and Greek lexicons, dictionaries, encyclopedias, commentaries, history books, and other writings. After finding the meaning or meanings of a particular word, its use in different scripture passages is considered. Additional help is gained from the renderings of various Bible translations.

It is my purpose in this treatise to show that the common assumption that fermented wine is the intended meaning of every Hebrew, Chaldee and Greek word in the Bible rendered "wine" cannot stand up under an examination of the use of those words. At times such a rendering cannot possibly be so, for in many instances the word is referring to the grape in its cluster on the vine. At times the word may refer to the grapes in the vat while the juice is being pressed out. There are times when the word rendered "wine" means dried raisins or raisin cakes. Or the word may refer to the fresh juice or must running into the lower vat during the pressing. Other meanings also may be indicated, such as the fresh unfermented juice being put into wineskins, the juice boiled into a thick syrup, the juice further cooked until it has become a thick jam, and of course at times the word may mean fermented grape juice.

To say that whenever the word wine is used in the Bible it always means that which is fermented and intoxicating makes the Bible full of contradictions and causes it to lose its divine authority for God cannot contradict Himself.

Whenever disapproval, condemnation, warning, prohibition accompanies the word wine, it must be understood that fermented wine is indicated. When God's approval, blessings, sanctions are given to wine, it must be understood that the unfermented is intended. There is no other way of harmonizing the Scriptures dealing with the subject.

The pure juice of the grape is one of God's blessings given to man for his enjoyment, benefit and health, and God's sanction is on its use. Fermented wine is a product of corruption, and it has been a corruptor of mankind through the ages.

As we shall see in the following pages, the literal meaning of Proverbs 23:31 is: "Look not thou upon the wine when it is fermented."

For seven years this writer was on the lecturing staff of the Temperance League of Illinois, formerly known as the Anti-Saloon League. In 1949, I gave a series of radio broadcasts on the Bible and wine. These broadcasts were condensed and published in a 41 page booklet entitled "The Bible and Its Wines." This booklet was well received and widely circulated and has gone through eight printings, although given very little publicity or advertising.

However a treatise that size was not sufficient to deal with all the different aspects of the subject and it left many questions unanswered. Since its publication I have gone through thousands of pages of research. Publications long out of print and no longer available have providentially fallen into my hands containing information not found in any modern literature, but which must be considered in order to understand many statements in the Scriptures. I present the results of my further studies in this revised and enlarged treatise under the same name "The Bible and Its Wines."

— Charles Wesley Ewing, D.D.

Chapter 1

WHAT IS WINE?

"A definition is the beginning of knowledge," said Demosthenes. Socrates said, *"If you would converse with me, define your terms."*

In the study of what the Bible has to say about wine, we must have a true definition of the word. This must be the beginning of our search for the truth. What is the meaning of this word, and what did those men who gave us our first English translations of the Bible mean when they used it?

This question must be answered before we are ready to go any further in our study for this word is used to translate a dozen Hebrew words which have a variety of meanings and two Greek words, one of which is also a generic term. We must also keep in mind that through time and common usage the meaning of words may change. Hundreds of English words are used today whose meanings have changed from what they meant three and a half centuries ago when the King James Version was being prepared by the translators (1604-1611 A.D.).

The word wine is one of these words. At the beginning of the seventeenth century, the fresh, sweet, unfermented juice of the grape was wine.

The oldest dictionary this writer has been able to find is that of Nathan Bailey. In the Detroit Public Library, Antique Books Section, is the Fourth Edition of Bailey's "The New Universal English Dictionary of Words, and of Arts and Sciences," carefully corrected by Mr. Buchanan, and published in 1759. James Shedd, in his "Dictionaries and That Dictionary," says, "In 1730 Bailey published his large folio edition, which omits all proper names, mythology, and so on, and is the first example of a complete dictionary as we understand the word."

In Bailey's dictionary we find the meaning of the word wine as it was understood in the year 1730 A.D., and of course this would be the meaning of the word before then. The reader may be amazed to find that the word fermented is not used at all by Bailey in his definition.

Here is Bailey's definition exactly as I found it in his dictionary: "Natural WINE, is such as it comes from the grape, without any mixture or sophistication." This of course is unfermented, nonintoxicating grape juice. Nowhere does Bailey use the words ferment, fermented, fermentation, fermented juice, fermented wine.

In addition to the above, Bailey gives the following: "Adulterated WINE, is that wherein some drug is added to give it strength, fineness, flavour, briskness, or some other qualification. Prick'd or Eager WINE, is that tourned sourish. Sulphur'd WINE, is that put in casks wherein sulphur has been burnt, in order to fit it for keeping or for carrying by sea. Colour WINE,

1

is wine of a deep colour, serving to die those wines that are too pale. Chip WINE, is that poured on chips of beech wood to fine or soften it. Rape WINE, is wine put into a cask of fresh grapes picked in order to recover the strength, briskness, & c. that it had lost." No other definition of wine in any form or of any kind is given by Bailey.

In none of these definitions does Bailey use the word fermented. Grant that his definition of Colour WINE, Chip WINE, and Rape WINE may include that which is fermented, it cannot be denied that his definition of Natural WINE: "is such as it comes from the grape, without any mixture or sophistication," must include unfermented even if it does mean fermented. But notice the words "without any mixture," which would mean that nothing is added to it, and the words "or sophistication." What is the meaning of this word? The New American Encyclopedic Dictionary, Volume 4, says: "Sophisticate, v. t. [Low Lat. sophisticatus, pa. par. of sophistico = to corrupt, to adulterate; Fr. sophistiquer; Sp. sofisticar; Ital. sophisticare.] 1. To corrupt, to prevent, to wrest from the truth. 2. To adulterate; to make spurious by admixture."

The fresh, unfermented grape juice as it comes from the grape, not mixed with any other substance, not sophisticated, not corrupted, not fermented, is wine. Fermentation is corruption, sophistication. Bailey tells us that the juice as it comes from the grape and has not been corrupted, sophisticated is wine. This point must be kept in mind.

Other lexicographers contemporaneous with Bailey also defined the word wine similarly. John Kersey's "Dictionarium Anglo-Britannicum, or A General English Dictionary," published in London in 1708: "Wine, a Liquor made of the Juice of Grapes or other Fruits. Liquor or Liquour, anthing that is liquid; Drink, Juice, etc. Must, (L.) sweet Wine, newly press'd from the grape."

B. N. Defoe's "A Complete English Dictionary," published in London in 1735: "WINE, a Liquor made of the Juice of Grapes, or other fruit. LIQUOR, anything that is liquid: Drink, Juice, Water, &c."

Benjamin Martin's "Lingua Brittanica Reformata, or A New English Dictionary," published in 1748: "WINE, 1. the juice of the grape. 2. a liquor extracted from other fruits besides the grape. 3. the vapours of wine, as wine disturbs his reason. LIQUOR, or LIQUOUR, any liquid thing, as water, juice, drink, etc."

I am indebted to Pixley for the last three definitions. Here are four English dictionaries, all published before 1750 A.D., which are unanimous in showing that the juice of the grape is wine, none of them requiring the juice to be fermented in order to be wine. They also show that liquor refers to any kind of drink, fermentation being no requisite, and most is the sweet wine newly pressed from the grape. Pixley also states that he could not find any statement written before 1825 asserting that unfermented grape juice is not really wine. This is very significant for it shows that only in the last 150 years has the concept developed that grape juice must be fermented in order to be wine.

2

A hundred years before the publication of the first of these four dictionaries the King James Version of the Bible was being prepared (1604-1611). If these lexicographers understood that the unfermented juice of the grape was wine, then the translators of the King James Version must have understood the same. The freshly expressed, unfermented, nonintoxicating juice of the grape is wine. If that juice were permitted to ferment it would be wine that was fermented or fermented wine. But it was wine before fermentation or sophistication. If it were preserved without fermentation it would still be wine.

It is admitted that in recent years lexicographers began to alter the definition of wine. The change did not come all at once. It came gradually and over a period of time. Nevertheless it came. The first change was the introducing of the words fermented and unfermented. The next change was the omission of the word unfermented. When the change was complete wine became defined as the fermented juice of the grape only with no reference at all to unfermented grape juice. This is the definition given today in many of our modern dictionaries, which is a complete reversal of the original definition of the word.

This trend is clearly shown in the Third, Fifth and Seventh Editions of Merriam Webster's Collegiate Dictionaries which I have before me as I write. The Third Edition says: "Wine [AS. win, fr. L. vinum] 1. Fermented juice of grapes. 2. The fermented juice, or loosely, the unfermented juice of any fruit or plant, used as a beverage." Now notice the definition given in the Fifth Edition: "Wine. [AS. win, fr. L. vinum.] 1. Fermented juice of grapes. Wine is essentially a dilute solution of alcohol, to which its stimulating properties are due, together with small quantities of certain ethers and esters which impart its bouquet. Red wine is made allowing the juice of dark-colored grapes to ferment in contact with the skins so as to extract their coloring matter; wine made in other ways is yellow or colorless and is termed white wine. 2. The fermented, or, loosely the unfermented, juice of any fruit or plant used as a beverage; as, currant wine."

Now notice that the Seventh Edition makes no reference at all to unfermented juice: "Wine [ME win, fr. OE win; akin to OHG win wine; both fr. a prehistoric Gmc word borrowed fr. L vinum wine, of non-IE origin; akin to the source of Gk oinos wine] 1: fermented grape juice containing varying percentages of alcohol together with ethers and esters that give it bouquet and flavor 2: the usu. fermented juice of a plant product (as a fruit) used as a beverage 3: something that invigorates or intoxicates." No mention at all is made in this definition of unfermented grape juice. Anyone reading this definition alone, and having no access to any other dictionaries or information, would naturally assume that grape juice of necessity must be fermented in order to be wine.

These definitions are a far departure from the original meaning of wine as understood by the first lexicographers and the translators of the King James Version.

A similar change in the definition of wine is seen in the Funk & Wagnalls Dictionaries. Need we be surprised at the confusion and misunderstanding of Bible teaching on the subject when our modern dictionaries have departed so far from the original meaning of the word?

Funk & Wagnalls College Standard Dictionary condensed from their New Standard Dictionary, 1922 Edition, says that wine is the fermented grape juice and immediately adds that in more extended use it is the expressed juice of the grape whether it is fermented or unfermented. The definition then says that by extension wine is also the expressed juice of other fruits. In the 1936 Edition of Funk & Wagnalls Standard College Dictionary no mention at all is made of unfermented grape juice or unfermented juice of any other fruit. The Reader's Digest Great Encyclopedic Dictionary, Third Edition, was published in 1969. This includes Funk & Wagnalls Standard College Dictionary which states that wine is fermented grape juice with varying alcoholic percentages and makes no mention whatever of unfermented grape juice or any other kind of juice.

Funk & Wagnalls Standard Family Dictionary, 1961 Edition defines wine as the fermented juice of the grape and says that by extension it means the unfermented juice of fruits other than the grape. This allows other unfermented fruit juices to be wine, but does not allow unfermented grape juice to be wine.

Other dictionaries have taken the lead of Merriam Webster and Funk & Wagnalls and are similarly omitting any reference to unfermented grape juice as being wine. However, a few dictionaries still show that unfermented grape juice is wine, but the trend is on. I have consulted numbers of other dictionaries, abridged and unabridged, and have found this trend to alter the original meaning of wine.

Our main interest, however, is not what the word means today, but what it meant four centuries ago when the Bible was being translated into English. Regardless of its present meaning, it is clear from the oldest dictionaries available that the unfermented nonintoxicating juice of the grape was called wine and the translators of the King James Version and other early translations understood this. The Bible reader must recognize this or he will never clearly understand many passages of the Scriptures.

In our present study it will be seen that our English word wine is cognate to the Greek oinos and the Hebrew yain, and therefore is a generic term with multiple meanings such as: the grape in the cluster on the vine, the grape dried in the form of raisins, the juice of the grape as it hangs on the vine, the freshly expressed juice of the grape, grape juice boiled into a syrup, grape juice further cooked into a thick jam, and also the fermented juice of the grape. Whatever form the grape juice may be in, it is wine according to Biblical usage, and this will be established in our study. Unless this is understood, we shall be hopelessly confused by different passages in the Bible related to the subject.

This is where the study must begin. Once the true meaning of wine is understood the next step is to find the meaning of the Hebrew, Chaldee and Greek words that are translated by our word wine. Again we must deal with definitions. Actually, our entire study is one of definitions.

Because the "wine is fermented grape juice" theory is so widespread, it will be necessary to give what may appear to some as an over-abundance of evidence to establish our position, but the only way to confute the One Wine Theorists is to show that the overwhelming weight of scholarship is against them. That is the purpose of this treatise.

Chapter 2

THE NECESSITY OF UNDERSTANDING ANCIENT CUSTOMS AND EXPRESSIONS

A mere cursory look at a few Bible verses is sufficient to show that, unless we have a true understanding of certain Hebrew, Chaldee and Greek words and idioms, nothing but confusion will prevail on our subject. To illustrate, let us consider a few passages.

"Look not thou upon the wine when it is red, when it giveth his colour in the cup, when it moveth itself aright." (Prov. 23:31). "And thou shalt bestow that money for whatsoever they soul lusteth after, for oxen, or for sheep, or for wine, or for strong drink" (Deut. 14:26). "Wine is a mocker, strong drink is raging, and whosoever is deceived thereby is not wise (Prov. 20:1). "Drink no longer water, but use a little wine for they Stomach's sake and thine often infirmities" (1 Tim. 5:25). "Should I leave my wine, which cheereth God and man" (Jud. 9:13)? "It is not for kings, O Lemuel, it is not for kings to drink wine; nor for princes strong drink: Lest they drink, and forget the law, and pervert the judgement of any of the afflicted" (Prov. 31:4,5). "Come ye, buy, and eat; yea, come, buy wine and milk without money and without price" (Isa. 55:1). "Woe unto him that giveth his neighbour drink, that puttest thy bottle to him" (Hab. 2:15). "Thus saith the Lord God of Israel, Every bottle shall be filled with wine" (Jer. 13:12). "Do not drink wine nor strong drink" (Lev. 10:9).

Certainly these few verses ought to be sufficient to demonstrate that, unless we are willing to concede that the Bible contradicts itself and cannot be relied upon as the infallible Word of God, we must know more about the true meaning of Bible terms and customs.

To do this we must keep in mind that we are dealing with writings that are from nineteen hundred to thirty-five hundred years old, writings which are expressions of an Oriental people who spoke different languages than we speak, whose customs were quite different from ours, and who used expressions peculiar to their customs which they clearly understood but which we may not use or understand in our day.

The languages used by these people were the ancient Hebrew, Chaldee and Koine Greek. These languages had idiomatic expressions which at times meant something entirely different from what those expressions mean to us two to three and a half milleniums later. Our search is for the true meaning, not of modern English words, but of ancient Hebrew, Chaldee and Greek words which have been translated into English, and at times it has been difficult for the translators to arrive at a proper rendering.

On the other hand, some scriptures are so clear that just an ordinary understanding of modern English and a thoughtful consideration of the

7

verse itself is all that is necessary to arrive at the true meaning.

"Look not upon the wine when. . ." (Prov. 23:31). Solomon here tells us as clearly as words are capable of conveying a meaning that there is a time "when" wine is not to be used, and of course the implication is that there is a time "when" wine may be taken.

The word when means "at what or which time; at the time that; while." "Look not thou upon the wine when it is red, when it giveth his colour in the cup, when it moveth itself aright." This is a description of wine "when" it is fermented, and it is "at the time that" it is fermented wine is not to be looked upon. "At the time that it moveth itself aright." This is fermentation. The meaning here is: "Look not thou upon the wine when it is fermented." If it does not give his colour in the cup, if it does not move itself aright (is not fermented), this prohibition does not apply.

This verse alone is sufficient to establish the fact that the Bible speaks of a wine that is fermented and a wine that is not fermented. The One Wine Theorists ignore this point. The entire context, verses 29 to 35, shows that it is fermented wine described here: "Who hath woe? who hath sorrow? who hath contentions? who hath babbling? who hath wounds without cause? who hath redness of eyes? They that tarry long at the wine; they that go to seek mixed wine. Look not thou upon the wine when it is red, when it giveth his colour in the cup, when it moveth itself aright. At the last it biteth like a serpent, and stingeth like an adder. Thine eyes shall behold strange women, and thine heart shall utter perverse things. Yea, thou shalt be as he that lieth down in the midst of the sea, or as he that lieth upon the top of a mast. They have stricken me, shalt thou say, and I was not sick; they have beaten me, and I felt it not: when shall I awake: I will seek it yet again."

Only fermented wine is indicated here. The freshly expressed or preserved grape juice, unfermented wine, does not produce the effects described in this passage: sorrow, contentions, babbling, wounds without cause, redness of eyes, the bite of a serpent, the sting of an adder, attraction to strange women, use of foul language, insensibility to pain, and alcoholic addition — seeking wine again after a bout of drunkenness. Only fermented wine is indicated here, wine that is in its "when" stage. Solomon says not to look upon wine when (at the time that) it is giving its colour in the cup, and is moving itself aright.

"Wine is a mocker, strong drink is raging: and whosoever is deceived thereby is not wise" (Prov. 20:1). Fresh unfermented wine is not a mocker. It is not raging. It is not a deceiver. It is a healthful, safe, beneficial food and brings no grief to those who use it.

"It is not for kings, O Lemuel, it is not for kings to drink wine; nor for princes strong drink; Lest they drink and forget the law, and pervert the judgement of any of the afflicted" (Prov. 31:4,5). Here is a plea for abstinence from fermented wine. Sweet grape juice, unfermented wine, would not cause the king to forget the law and pervert judgement.

These passages can be understood without reference to Hebrew lexicons. Neither is an English dictionary needed. On the other hand, the full meaning of the following verse cannot be understood without a definition of one or two Hebrew words: "Woe unto him that giveth his neighbor drink, that puttest thy bottle to him, and makest him drunken also" (Hab. 2:15). Here a curse is pronounced upon the man that gives drink to his neighbor, but what kind of drink? The full import of this verse is lost in the King James Version. Dawson Burns has shown that the word bottle should be "poison" making the verse read "that puttest thy poison to him." The Hebrew word is "khamah." This is confirmed by Young's Analytical Concordance and other Hebrew scholars. The Hebrew word for drink in this verse is "shaqah" which Strong defines as: "a Prim. root; to quaff, i.e. (caus.) to irrigate or furnish a potion to:-cause to (give, give to, let, make to) drink, drown, moisten, water."

So that no one would mistake his meaning of the word drink the prophet immediately specifies what kind is meant: the kind that is "poison," a fermented drink which "maketh him drunken." Giving this kind of drink has a curse pronounced upon it.

Burns says: "In referring to strong drink there is a remarkable use of 'khamah,' a word translated in the English version 'poison,' 'anger,' 'fury,' 'heat'; but the sense of which is lost in two important passages, where the colorless rendering 'bottle' is given to it. In Hosea vii,5, 'the princes have made him sick with bottles of wine,' should be, by consent of all critics, 'the princes have made him sick with poison (or inflaming heat) of wine.' And in Habakkuk ii,15, 'that puttest thy bottle to him,' should be 'that puttest thy poison (or inflaming drink) to him.' The same word occurs in Deut. 32,33 'Their wine is the poison (Khamath) of dragons': a text which throws light on Prov. xxiii.32, where the red bubbling wine is compared to the serpent."

F. R. Lees, commenting on Hab. 2:15 says, "Such drink is called a 'poison,' a 'deceiver,' a 'mocker,' and a 'defrauder' ('treacherous dealer' in R.V.). The first and last time in which chemeh, the generic Hebrew term for 'poison' occurs, it is applied to intoxicating wine; and in descriptive passages the drink of the drunkard is in fact declared to be a narcotic brain-poison, and a paralyzer of the will. 'They have beaten me, and I felt it not . . . I will seek it yet again.' The word for 'poison' has a metaphorical use in accordance with the literal. It is the word which characterizes the contents of the 'cup of wrath,' and is expressive of the divine punishment upon sin (Jer. 25:15, etc.). It was not a 'cup of blessing'; and the toxic quality is the whole point and meaning of the figure, so in the 14th chapter of the Apocalypse, in which book the philosophy of Prohibition is also distinctly taught. The binding of Satan precedes the millenium of purity and peace. The divine kingdom is always conditioned upon deliverance from evil and from the pressure of perpetual temptation" (Cyclopedia of Temperance and Prohibition).

The following translations confirm the position of Burns and Lees on Hab. 2:15. Fenton: "Woe! to you who give drink to your friends! You who pour out your poison to them." I. M. Rubin: "Woe unto him that maketh his neighbor drink, that pourest out, poison, and maketh them also drunken." Moffatt: "Woe to him who makes his neighbours drain the goblet of his fury, and makes them drunk." New Catholic Bible: "Woe to him that giveth drink to his friend, and presenteth his gall, and maketh him drunk." Isaac Leeser: "Woe unto him that maketh his neighbor drink, (to thee) that pourest out

9

thy poisonous (wine) and makest them also drunken." Rotherham: "Alas! for him who causeth his neighbor to drink, From the goblet of they fury and also making him drunk." American Standard Version: "Woe unto him that giveth his neighbor drink, to thee that addest thy venom, and makest him drunken also." Footnote uses the word "fury." English Revised Version: "Woe unto him that giveth his neighbour drink, that addest thy venom thereto, and makest him drunken also." Marginal note says "fury." Revised Standard Version: "Woe to him who makes his neighbor drink of the cup of his wrath and makes them drunk." Lamsa: "Woe to him who makes his neighbor drink the dregs of fury."

These translations show that the Bible declares intoxicating wine is a poison. Nowhere do the Scriptures speak of sweet grape juice, unfermented wine as a poison. Any drink that contains alcohol is a poison.

Dr. Andrew C. Ivy, in his "Definition of Terms Basic to the Problems Created by the Consumption of Alcohol" says: "Alcohol, from a pharmacological and medical viewpoint, is an intoxicating, hypnotic, analgesic, anesthetic, poisonous, and potentially habit-forming, craving-producing or addiction-producing drug."

Any beverage that contains alcohol contains poison. Fermented wine contains alcohol, a poison, an intoxicant, a hypnotic, an analgesic, an anesthetic, a potentially habit-forming, craving-producing, addiction-producing drug. To this writer, it is inconceivable that an all-wise God, with the best interests of His creatures in mind, would give His sanction to the use of any drink that contains poison, or that is an addiction-producing drug.

I have not found one writer among the Moderationists who comments on or even acknowledges the fact that the Bible in Hab. 2:15; Hosea 7:5 and Deut. 32:33 states that fermented wine is poison.

Just as the Hebrew word "khamah" (poison) in Hab. 2:15 must be properly defined to rightly understand the verse, there are other Hebrew and Greek words that must also be similarly defined if we are to rightly understand other passages of the Scriptures. For this reason a considerable amount of this treatise consists of definitions of Biblical words, idioms and terminology, and the explanation of ancient customs and usages.

Chapter 3

YAYIN — GRAPES, RAISINS, SYRUP, JAM, UNFERMENTED AND FERMENTED WINE

Yayin (also yain), is used in the Bible more than any other Hebrew word dealing with our subject. Young lists 131 references for Yayin. Strong gives 136. Douglas says it appears 141 times, and the Companion Bible says 142.

Yayin along with tirosh and shekar in the Old Testament, and oinos in the New Testament and in the Septuagint Greek Old Testament are the four most important, most used, and most misunderstood words in the Bible dealing with wine and strong drink. Practically all of the confusion on the subject is due to an improper or incomplete definition of these words and a failure to see that all four of them are generic terms and are used in the Scriptures to designate different products of the vine and tree.

Hebraists who have made a thorough study of this word state that it is a generic term meaning: the grapes in the cluster on the vine; dried grapes or raisins; the juice in the grape still hanging on the vine; the freshly expressed and unfermented juice of the grape; grape juice that is boiled to prevent fermentation so it can be bottled for storage; the juice boiled until it becomes a thick syrup to be kept for future use; the juice cooked into a thicker jam to preserve it for future use when it and also the syrup, was mixed with water or milk for drinking or spread on bread; and grape juice that has fermented and is intoxicating.

One of the meanings of yayin is fermented wine. This is readily conceded. But it is ridiculous to assume that what a generic word means in one text is must invariably mean in everyone of 140 other texts where it is used. Nevertheless, this is the manner of Bible interpretation used by One Wine Theorists who teach that wine is always fermented and there is no such thing as unfermented wine. I was amazed to find that Bullinger's Companion Bible takes this position in its Appendix 27: "With these data it will be seen that the modern expression, 'unfermented wine,' is a contradiction of terms. If it is wine, it must have fermented. If it is not fermented, it is not wine, but a syrup." Mr. Bullinger failed to explain how the term "unfermented wine" originated, but it is clear that in his day there were those who held that wine did not have to be fermented in order to be called wine.

It further amazed me to read Howard Crosby's words about Paul's advice to Timothy in his "Reasons Against the Unfermented Wine Theory." Crosby wrote: "He (Paul) did not know that there was a non-intoxicating wine." This is to say that Paul had never been informed that grape juice could be taken before it became fermented, or that unfermented grape syrup or jam was especially used, mixed with water, by persons with dyspeptic stomachs and was known as "stomach wine" or "wine for the stomach." But this will be dealt with more fully later.

11

The following writers show that our English word wine derives from the Hebrew yayin (yain) and is a generic word with several meanings even as yayin has several meanings.

Davies shows that the English word wine derives from the Hebrew "yain" as does the Greek "oinos;" the Ethiopian "wain;" Armenian "gini;" Latin "vinum;" German "wein;" Welsh "gwin;" Gaelic "fion."

The New American Encyclopedic Dictionary gives four spellings for the English word wine, three of which are now archaic, "win, wyn, wyne," and gives the corresponding word in ten languages: Anglo-Saxon "win;" Latin "vinum;" Gothic "wein:" Old High German "win;" Icelandic "vin;" Dutch "wign;" Swedish "vin;" Danish "viin;" Greek "oinos;" Old Irish "fin."

Our English word vine (old spelling vyne) derives from the Greek oine — the vine.

The American Ecclesiastical Review, in 1898, defined yayin: "Yayin is wine generally, new or old, fermented or unfermented, but usually the latter. The Hebrew YOD (consonant) in the beginning of a word answers to a W in the related languages, and the word for wine is actually the same in Hebrew, Latin, Greek, English and several other languages, with but a slight difference in pronunciation" (Pixley's Review and Comments).

The following comments on the Hebrew yayin and the Greek oinos by Ferrar Fenton of England are very illuminating. Fenton cannot be taken lightly for he was one of the Church's great scholars of Biblical languages. By the time he was 28 years old, he had acquired a working knowledge of 25 classical, Oriental and modern languages. So he was at home with the languages of the Bible. In fact, Fenton spent 40 years studying the Bible in its original languages before attempting to give the world his own translation of the Scriptures. It is regrettable that his book "The Bible and Wine" is no longer published.

Fenton says: Oinon, the fruit of the Vine or Grape-plant. It is also used to denote various kinds of drinks or confections of other succulent fruits, such as Date or Lotus fruit, according to Liddell and Scott's lexicon. According to Professor Samuel Lee, of Cambridge University, the root of the Greek word is undoubtedly the Hebrew vocable, Yain, Wine; which, as I have before shown, under the sections of my essay devoted to the philology of that Hebrew noun, was not confined to an intoxicating liquor made from fruits by alcoholic fermentation of their expressed juices, but more frequently referred to a thick, non-intoxicating Syrup, Conserve, or Jam, produced by boiling, to make them storable as articles of food, exactly as we do at the present day. The only difference being that we store them in jars, bottles, or metal cans, whilst the Ancients laid them up in skin bottles, as Aristotle and Pliny, and other classic writers upon agricultural and household affairs describe. Consequently the contention of some of my Correspondents that the Greek Oinos always meant fermented and intoxicating liquor is totally inaccurate, and only arises from ignorance, or prejudice in favour of the delusion of Commentators of the Dark Ages, who fancied Drunkenness was the highest delight, and Intoxication an imperative Christian practice; because Mohammedan Arabians were a sober people.

"Oine, and Oinon, the Grape, or Vine-Plant. Oinos, Wine, or drink made from any fruit or grain, such as dates, apples, pears, barley, the lotus seed. If specially indicated as made from Grapes it is called Oinos 'ampelinos.'

"As in the Hebrew "yain," the word does not in Greek always signify fermented intoxicating drink, but Grapes as fresh fruit, dried as raisins, or prepared as Jam, or preserved by boiling for storage, or as thick syrup dissolved in water for a beverage at meals, as described in the Hebrew Bible by Solomon and others, and amongst Greek writers by Aristotle, and Pliny amongst the Roman ones. This mixing of the syrup with water ready for use at meals is alluded to in more than one of Our Lord's Parables. The liquor was absolutely non-alcoholic and not intoxicating. Grape-juice was also prepared by heating it, as soon as possible after it had been squeezed in the press, by boiling, so as to prevent fermentation, and yet preserve its thin liquid form as a drink. To ensure this certain resinous gums were dissolved in the juice, or sulphate of lime, or what it commonly called gypsum, was put into it, as is now done in Spain, to make the liquid clear and bright, and prevent subsequent fermentation arising from changes of atmosphere. . .

"It should never be forgotten that when reading the Bible and the classic pagan writers of 'Wine,' we are seldom dealing with the strongly intoxicating and loaded liquids to which that name is alone attached in the English language, but usually with beverages such as above described. They were as harmless and sober as our own Teas, Coffees, and Cocoas. Had they not been so, the ancient populations would have been perpetually in a more or less state of drunkenness, for they had none of our above-noted herb-made drinks to use as a part of their dietary. These facts should never be forgotten when we read of 'Wine' there, — for it was simple fruit syrup, except where especially stated to be of the intoxicating kinds, which latter the Prophets and Legislators always condemned."

Young and Strong do not agree in their definitions of yayin. Young merely defines it as: "What is pressed out, grape juice." Strong says the word is: "from an unused root mean. to effervesce; wine (as fermented); by impl. intoxication." Neither of these definitions is sufficient for the word includes both the fresh grape juice and the fermented, although the effervescence is not necessarily the result of fermentation but more especially the foaming that results from the running of the juice from the upper vat into the lower during the pressing of the grapes, as we shall see later.

Burns says: "What, then, are the facts patent to every careful reader? When Yayin — the generic term for expressed juice of the grape — is described as a blessing, it is never represented as having an intoxicating quality, but as the liquor (in one place, Jer. x1.1, 12, as the solid) produce of the vine."

Douglas, in Fairbairn's Imperial Standard Bible Encyclopedia, says: "The general word for the produce of the vine, when this has been transformed into a liquid, is yayin, 'wine,' derived according to the prevalent opinion from a root meaning 'to be turbid, to boil up,' and applied to the grape-juice as it rushes foaming into the wine-vat. Others consider it to be a word foreign to the Jews, and the nations who spoke kindred languages: certainly the word is found to be very widespread, as in the Greek oinos, the

Latin vinum, etc. This Hebrew word is said to occur 141 times in the Old Testament, and the Greek word 32 times in the New, besides words derived from it. It seems to be used to describe 'all sorts of wine,' Ne. 5. 18, from the simple grape juice, or a thickened syrup, to the strongest liquors with which the Israelites were acquainted, the use of which often led to deplorable scenes of drunkenness. As to the particular kinds of wine in use, our information is very scanty. The wine of Helbon is mentioned, Exe. xxvii. 18, as much esteemed (see Helbon), and the same may have been the case with the wine of Lebanon, Ho. xiv. 8 (7, English Version)."

Fausset: "Yayin, from a root 'boil up,' is the extract from the grape, whether simple juice unfermented, or intoxicating wine; akin to the Gr. oinos, Latin vinum. Vinum, vitis are thought akin to Sanskrit we, 'weave,' viere." Thus Fausset also shows that yayin means either the sweet unfermented juice or the fermented.

Hitt writes: "Yah-yin, or Greek oinos, occurs about 140 times, and is a very general term, meaning unfermented fruit juices probably as often as fermented wine, just as the Latin vinum was used as a general term."

The Jewish Encyclopedia says: "Fresh wine before fermentation was called 'yayin-mi-gat' (wine of the vat; Sanh. 70a) . . ." (Article by Judah David Eisenstein, Vol. 12, p. 533). Here is proof from Jewish authority that yayin is not always used to signify fermented grape juice, and also that the juice before fermenting is wine.

McClintock and Strong say: "As to the exclusively liquid character of the substance denoted, both yayin and tirosh are occasionally connected with expressions that would apply properly to a fruit; the formerly, for instance, with verbs significant of gathering (Jer. x1, 10, 12) and growing (Psa. civ. 14, 15); the latter with gathering (Isa. lxii, 8, 9, A.V. 'brought it together'), treading (Mic. vi, 15), and withering (Isa. xxxiv, 7; Joel i, 10). So again the former is used in Numb. vi, 4 to define the particular kind of tree whose products were forbidden to the Nazarite, viz. the 'pendulous shoot of the vine;' and the latter in Judges ix, 13 to denote the product of the vine" (Encyclopedia of Biblical and Ecclesiastical Literature, Vol. 10). This confirms Fenton's position that yayin at times refers to the fruit itself, the grape on the vine.

To the above could be added the statements of many other Hebraists who say that yayin is a multiple meaning word and cannot be limited to the definition of fermented wine only. But why add more to what is enough?

"We have also a more sure word of prophecy; whereunto ye do well that ye take heed, as unto a light that shineth in a dark place" (2 Pet. 1:19). Old Testament prophets used the word yayin in ways that cannot be interpreted as meaning intoxicating, fermented wine. If we can find just one instance in the Bible where yayin is used in a sense that means something other than fermented wine our point will be proved. This we shall proceed to do, not with just one instance but with several.

Isa. 16:10, "And gladness is taken away, and joy out of the plentiful field, and in the vineyards there shall be no singing, neither shall there be shouting: the treaders shall tread no wine (yayin) in their presses; I have made their vintage shouting to cease." By no stretch of the imagination can the word yayin in this verse be interpreted as fermented, alcoholic wine. It can only mean the grapes as they are being crushed under the feet of the treaders, or the fresh juice as it is pressed from the grapes. Fermented, alcoholic wine is not pressed from the grapes. It takes many days for complete fermentation to take place, but the figure here is the immediate pressing of the juice from the grapes. The use of the word yayin here is proof that the grape itself, or the fresh juice just pressed from the grapes is yayin, wine.

Jer. 40:10, "As for me, I will dwell at Mizpeh, to serve the Chaldeans, which will come unto us: but ye, gather ye wine (yayin), and summer fruits, and oil and put them in your vessels, and dwell in your cities that ye have taken." Men do not go into the vineyards and gather fermented wine. They gather grapes, and that is the meaning of yayin here.

Jer. 40:12, "Even all the Jews returned out of all places whither they were driven, and came to the land of Judah, to Gedaliah, unto Mizpeh, and gathered wine (yayin) and summer fruits very much." Again the meaning of yayin here is grapes. This is also established by the fact that the yayin was gathered at the same time summer fruits were gathered. It was a harvesting of the produce of the vineyard and of the orchard. Alcoholic wine is not gathered, it is fermented.

Jer. 48:32,33, "O vin of Sibmah, I will weep for thee with the weeping of Jazar: the spoiler is fallen upon they summer fruits and upon they vintage. And joy and gladness is taken from the plentiful field, and from the land of Moab; and I have caused wine (yayin) to fail from the winepresses: none shall tread with shouting; their shouting shall be no shouting." The prophet here is describing the conditions that will be after the spoiling of the fruits, vintage and fields: no fruits in the orchards, no grains in the field, no grapes in the vineyard. Consequently, there would be no grapes to tread in the winepresses. "I have caused wine (yayin) to fail from the winepresses, none shall tread with shouting." The use of yayin here shows that in ancient times the grapes in the vineyard and the grapes in the vat to be pressed were called yayin, wine.

Micah 6:15, "Thou shalt sow, but thou shalt not reap; thou shalt tread the olives, but thou shalt not anoint thee with oil; and sweet wine (tirosh), but shalt not drink wine (yayin). As we shall see later, one of the meanings of tirosh is the grape in the cluster; and we have already seen that one of the meanings of yayin is "what is pressed out, grape juice," the only definition given by Young. The use of both words in this sentence gives a literal rendering: "Thou shalt tread grapes (tirosh), but shalt not drink what is pressed out (yayin)." This is in complete harmony with the definitions of both tirosh and yayin.

The above scriptures show that the word yayin, translated wine, does not always mean a fermented, intoxicating drink. It means grapes, grape products, and unfermented wine as well as fermented.

Unless this point is understood, we find the Bible both condemning and sanctioning the use of intoxicants. In those passages where yayin is condemned, prohibited or associated with warnings and curses, it must be

15

understood to mean the fermented kind. Where it is spoken of as being beneficial to health and happiness, and God's approval is upon it, we must understand it to mean that which is unfermented. Any other position robs the Bible of its infallibility and adds confusion to contradiction.

When the King James Translators, three hundred seventy years ago, were preparing their translation, they used the word wine for yayin. Why? Did they do it in ignorance? Did they not know that yayin was a generic word with fermented wine as only one of its several meanings? Or did they know what is not commonly known today that the English word wine derives from yayin and is also a generic word with the same meaning that its mother word has, fermented being only one of those meanings? This is the only explanation for the consistent use of our English wine for the Hebrew yayin.

Our problem in the twentieth century is that we do not know the full meaning of the word wine, and use it only in the sense of something fermented.

On the basis of the etymology of the word itself, the meaning of the mother-word from which it derives, the employment of the word in the King James and other Versions, the definition given in the early English dictionaries, the meaning of the word still given in some modern dictionaries, this writer unhesitatingly declares that, according to ancient practice and the manner in which the word is used in the Bible:

The grapes in the cluster on the vine ready to be gathered are wine. The grapes in the vat to be pressed are wine. The foaming fresh juice of the grapes pouring from the press into the lower vat is wine. The juice of the grapes boiled in preparation for bottling is wine. Preserved unfermented grape juice is wine. Grape syrup is wine. Grape jam is wine. Grapes dried and pressed into a raisin cake are wine. Grape juice which has fermented, becoming alcoholic and intoxicating is wine. All these definitions will be further established as we study other Hebrew and Greek words that the word wine has been used to translate.

It matters not what the word has been reduced to mean in the last quarter of the twentieth century. I am aware of the fact that my position is not the popular one, but I can never forget the sage advice given me thirty years ago by an elderly retired Methodist minister who was correcting me on my pronunciation of the saith, pronounced "seth," not "sayeth." In my radio broadcasting I used the wrong pronunciation. I said, "Everybody says say-eth." Dr. Hall gave me the challenge, "Will you dare to be right?" His admonition has stuck with me through these years, and I dare to state my position, unpopular though it be, that our English word wine, derived from the Hebrew yayin, is a generic term and fermented grape juice is only one of its several meanings.

Chapter 4

TIROSH — UNFERMENTED WINE, THE FRUIT OF THE VINE

Tirosh (also spelled tiyrosh, tiyrowsh, thirosh, teerosche, teerosh) is found in 38 texts of the Old Testament. Unlike the generic word yayin, it has a limited meaning and never carries the sense of anything fermented or intoxicating. Because of our misunderstanding of the word wine used to translate tirosh, it like yayin is believed to be an intoxicant. This could not be further from the truth.

Tirosh is never associated with debauchery, neither is its use condemned by the prophets as yayin is at times. It is used in association with the produce of the field and of the orchard; is represented as one of God's blessings upon Israel; and is wholesome and beneficial to those who use it.

The meaning of tirosh is vintage fruit or fruit of the vine. It also means the juice of the grape in the cluster, the freshly expressed grape juice, must, and the preserved unfermented juice, but never fermented.

Some writers, in their zeal to defend fermented wine, have written that tirosh is rendered new wine because it gets possession of the brain so quickly. I do not know who was the first to come up with this but I found the statement in Bullinger's Companion Bible, Appendix 29, and other writers have said the same. New wine has no intoxicating effect at all being the freshly expressed grape juice, the reason for the word new.

Fermentation is the process whereby yeast germs eat the sugar in the fresh juice and throw off alcohol and carbon dioxide. It takes several weeks before fermentation is complete and the percentage of alcohol in the wine reaches its highest percentage, not more than fourteen percent. The grape juice freshly pressed from the grape contains no alcohol. That is the reason for calling it new.

It is neither the newness nor the oldness of wine that causes intoxication, gets possession of the brain. It is the alcohol that intoxicates. The degree of intoxication depends upon the amount of alcohol in the bloodstream. The higher the percentage of alcohol in the blood, the more the intoxication, the more the brain will be affected. The alcohol-blood saturation depends on several factors: the percent of alcohol in the drink, the size and weight of the drinker, the amount consumed, the time taken to consume the alcohol, whether it is taken on an empty or full stomach, etc. All these factors are involved in the degree of intoxication, getting possession of the brain. Tirosh is not called new wine because it intoxicates so quickly but because it is fresh or new grape juice, not fermented.

Judah David Eisenstein, writing in the Jewish Encyclopedia, says ". . .'tirosh' includes all kinds of sweet juices and must and does not include

17

fermented wine. (tosef., Ne. iv,3)." The Jewish Encyclopedia is an authority on this point that must not be ignored. The word tirosh is rendered wine, new wine, sweet wine by the King James Translators in every verse that it appears in the Old Testament simply because they understood that the English word has all the meaning that both Hebrew words yayin and tirosh have.

The New Schaff-Herzog Encyclopedia of Religious Knowledge says, "The usual designation for fermented grape juice is yayin, a loan-word in the Hebrew corresponding to Greek Oinos and Latin vinum; tirosh is used to denote the newly extracted grape juice (Lat. mustum; cf. Mic. vi,15) and also the juice yet contained in the cluster (Isa. lxv, 80)."

Samson says, "The entire history of translations, of renderings by lexicographers and of Hebrew and Oriental Christian commentators, confirms the belief that tirosh is unfermented wine. Fuerst, the latest and best archeological lexicographer, renders it ungegorener Wein, 'unfermented wine'".

William Gesenius also says that tirosh is ungegorener Wein in his Hebrew German Lexicon.

All modern Hebraists recognize the works of Gesenius and Fuerst (also Furst) very highly and many Hebrew lexicographers base their writings upon the works of these two men. So their definitions of tirosh as ungegorener Wein (unfermented wine) are of great significance.

It is tragic that some English editions of Gesenius' lexicon have not properly translated his definition of tirosh as Most, ungegorener Wein (must, unfermented wine), but it is indisputable that Gesenius himself gave this definition in his German work.

In the years 1810-1812, Gesenius' Hebrew-German Hand Dictionary of the Scriptures of the Old Testament was published. Three years later an abridgement of this was published which was followed by sixteen editions of this abridgement. In all, 18 editions of Gesenius' lexicon have been published, the last being in 1912, and this was reprinted in 1949 and again in 1954. Victor A. Pixley, who has done excellent research on this subject, went through every edition of Gesenius and found that without exception they all define tirosh as Most, ungegorener Wein.

Regardless of the fact that Gesenius' translators have failed to translate tirosh as unfermented wine, and regardless of the fact that those who consult their translations are led to believe that Gesenius did not render it so, his original German work and every reprint of it defined tirosh as Most, ungegorener Wein.

McClintock and Strong's Cyclopedia of Biblical, Theological and Ecclesiastical Literature says: "Tirosh . . . 'sweet wine,' (in Mic. vi. 15) properly signifies must, the freshly pressed juice of the grape (the gleukos, or sweet wine of the Greeks, rendered 'new wine' in Acts ii.13)." McClintock and Strong further say: "As to the exclusively liquid character of the substance denoted, both yayin and tirosh are occasionally connected with expressions that would apply properly to a fruit; the formerly for instance, with verbs significant of gathering (Jer. xl, 10, 12) and growing (Psa. civ, 14, 15); the latter with gathering (Isa. lxii, 9, A.V. 'brought it together'), treading (Mic.

vi, 15), and withering (Isa. xxxiv, 7; Joel i, 10), so again the former is used in Numb. vi, 4 to define the particular kind of tree whose products were forbidden to the Nazarite, viz. the 'pendulous shoot of the vine' and the latter in Judges ix, 13 to denote the product of the vine."

Lees says, "Tirosh is a collective term for 'the fruit of the vine' in its natural state, from the early 'tirosh in the cluster' to the richer 'blessing within it' of the full ripe grapes, ready for grateful consumption. Hence, Micah's phrase, 'Thou shalt tread vine fruit (tirosh), but shall not drink yayin,' for the fruit shall be withered (vi,15). It is associated, as a thing of growth, with corn, and orchard fruit (yitzhar — not oil); dependent upon the dew and rain" (Text Book of Temperance).

Burns writes similarly: "Tirosh, often spoken of in connection with corn and oil (Yitzhar — orchard fruit) is represented as growing upon the vine, and was the name for vintage fruit. It is distinctly spoken of (Mic. vi. 15) as trodden, and thus yielding Yayin. Only once is it referred to as possibly a liquid (Isaiah lxii. 8) and this apparent exception is explicable as an idiom, as when we speak of 'drinking a cup,'" meaning its contents. The triad of dahgan (corn), Tirosh (vine fruit), and yitzhar (olive and orchard fruit), comprehend the whole of that agricultural wealth which Israel held on the tenure of loyal obedience to the Great King."

Whether a liquid or a solid, these Hebraists agree that tirosh does not mean something fermented.

Faussett says: "Tirosh is the most general term for 'vintage fruit,' put in connection with 'corn and oil,' necessaries (dagan, yitzhar, rather more generally the produce of the field and the orchard) and ordinary articles of diet in Palestine. It occurs 38 times, viz. six times by itself, eleven times with dagan, twice with yitzhar, nineteen times with both dagan and yitzhar. Besides it is seven times with 'firstfruits', ten times with 'tithes or offerings' of fruits and grain; very rarely with terms expressing the process of preparing fruits or vegetable produce." Faussett then gives a list of scripture verses which we shall consider later.

Hitt writes: "Hebrew — Tee-rosche means vintage fruit, or fruit of the vine."

Douglas brings out the same facts that Faussett does: "The most general word, then, among those applied to the produce of the vine is tirosh, which we translate 'vintage fruit.' In the Authorized Version and in others, this meaning is not found; the common renderings being 'wine,' and 'new wine,' though also 'sweet wine,' Mi. vi. 15; all which in reality are translations of words to be subsequently noticed. The force of the argument for rendering it 'vintage fruit,' is seen expecially (1.) when we observe how it is habitually combined with dagan and yitzhar, translated 'corn and oil' in the Authorized Version, but which are to be taken in a very wide or generic sense, the former as including all kinds of grain, and the latter as meaning 'orchard fruit,' though in this a prominent place may have been given to the fruit of the olive, from which oil (shemen) was extracted."

Douglas then gives the same information that Faussett gives about the number of times that tirosh (produce of the vine) occurs together with dagan (produce of the field), yitzhar (produce of the orchard), and with both dagan and yitzhar, and the number of times it occurs by itself. He then shows that tirosh is used seven times combined with the 'first-fruits', which were mainly the first of the gathered grain and fruits in their natural state. Like Douglas he gives a list of passages which we shall consider.

The arguments made by Lees, Faussett and Douglas have never been answered, and I have not found one person among the One Wine Theorists who give evidence of having so much as read Judah David Eisenstein's statement in the Jewish Encyclopedia. Burns lists 37 references where the word tirosh occurs and says that only once is it referred to as possibly a liquid (Isa. 1xii.8), and shows that this is an idiomatic expression.

The way tirosh is used in the Bible is in itself sufficient to establish that it does not mean fermented, even if we did not have the word of the above writers.

Deut. 11:14, ". . . that thou mayest gather in thy corn, and thy wine, and thine oil." Tirosh (wine) here means either the grapes in the cluster or the fresh juice that is in the grapes as they are gathered. Men do not gather fermented wine. Fermented wine is grape juice that has been permitted to set for some time while the yeast germs turn the sugar, which at times may be as much as thirty percent of the grape, into carbon dioxide and alcohol, which in the sweetest juices may become fourteen percent. The produce of the vine (tirosh) that men gather does not contain alcohol or carbon dioxide, and it does contain all of its original sugars. If it be argued that men do not gather oil, but the olives, we reply that the oil in the olive is the same as that which has been pressed out and it has not gone through the process of fermentation. Furthermore the word yitzhar, as the above writers have shown, is the fruit of the orchard.

Prov. 3:10, "So shall thy barns be filled with plenty, and thy presses shall burst out with wine (tirosh)." Most translations I have consulted say "overflow" instead of burst out. The promise is that of such a bountiful harvest that the barns will be completely filled, and the vats will not be able to hold the tirosh. This could mean either the grapes are so plentiful that the upper vat in which they are to be pressed cannot hold them, or the lower vat into which the juice pours is not large enough to contain it. The writer is dealing with the harvesting of that which is stored in the barns or cast into the vats for pressing. Tirosh here means either the grapes or the freshly expressed juice. The King James version actually says "thy presses shall burst out with new wine." New wine has not gone through the process of fermenting or aging. Ferrar Fenton's Translation says "fruit" instead of new wine, for tirosh is the fruit of the vine.

Isa. 65:8, "Thus saith the Lord, As the new wine (tirosh) is found in the cluster, and one saith, Destroy it not; for a blessing is in it: so will I do for my servant's sakes, that I may not destroy them all." Fermented wine contains alcohol and carbon dioxide and neither of these is found in the cluster. What is found in the cluster contains from fifteen to thirty percent sugar, but no sugar is retained in the fermented juice. Alcoholic drinks have been a curse to humanity throughout the centuries. But blessings are in that which is found in the cluster; it has God's approval; is given to us for food; and is beneficial to the health.

Joel 2:24, "And the floors shall be full of wheat, and the vats shall overflow with wine (tirosh) and oil." This is another promise of a plentiful harvest. The threshing floor is filled with wheat for threshing, and the vats cannot hold the grapes, they are so abundant, and the olive harvest is so great the vats cannot hold all the oil pressed from them. Notice particularly that the vats overflow. This is definitely a description of what takes place during the pressing of the grapes and olives. There is not the least of a suggestion here that the grape juice is going through the process of fermentation which takes time, even weeks to reach full conversion of the sugars into alcohol.

Joel 1:5,10, "Awake, ye drunkards, and weep; and howl, all ye drinkers of wine (yayin), because of the new wine (asis); for it is cut off from your mouth . . . The field is wasted, the land mourneth; for the corn is wasted: the new wine (tirosh) is dried up."

I have shown that yayin is a generic word meaning either fermented or unfermented wine. Asis means fresh juice as we shall see later. But our main interest here is the use of tirosh. All three words are used in this chapter which describes the condition of the land caused by the palmerworm, the locust, the cankerworm, and the caterpillar. A nation also went through the land causing more devastation to the fields, orchards and vineyards, and the drought produced more withering.

The drunkards and drinkers of wine (yayin) were to weep and howl, because the new wine (asis) was cut off from their mouths (the supply was gone), and the new wine (tirosh —fruit of the vine, grapes) dried up. "The new wine (tirosh) is dried up" can only refer to the grapes on the vine. It could not refer to the juice for that would have been put into bottles and the drought could not have affected it.

Isa. 62:8,9, "The Lord hath sworn by his right hand, and by the arm of his strength, Surely I will no more give thy corn (dagan) to be meat for thine enemies; and the sons of the stranger shall not drink thy wine (tirosh), for the which thou has labored: But they that have gathered it shall eat it, and praise the Lord; and they that have brought it together shall drink it in the courts of my holiness." Tirosh is used here to indicate a solid that is gathered, brought together, eaten, and something to drink. Only the grapes can be gathered from the vine, and I have shown from the above Hebraists that tirosh never is used for that which is fermented. The tirosh in these two verses to be drunk is the unfermented fruit of the vine, pure grape juice.

Micah 6:15, "Thou shalt sow, but thou shalt not reap; thou shalt tread the olives, but thou shalt not anoint thee with oil; and sweet wine (tirosh), but shalt not drink wine (yayin)." The use of tirosh here can only mean grapes. They were to tread something but not be allowed to drink that which the treading had produced. The verb tread was used for the olives and for the tirosh (produce of the vine). Tirosh here cannot mean anything else than the grapes. We explained this verse in Chapter 3.

Deut. 12:17, "Thou mayest not eat within thy gates the tithe of thy corn (dagan), or of thy wine (tirosh), or of thy oil (yitzhar), or the firstlings of thy

21

herds or of thy flocks, nor any of they vows which thou vowest, nor thy freewill offerings, or heave offerings of thine hand: But thou shalt eat them before the Lord thy God in the place which the Lord thy God shall choose." I have shown from the testimony of Burns, Faussett and Douglas that the Hebrew dagan and yitzhar are used in a more generic sense and mean produce of the field and produce of the orchard when mentioned as first-fruits or tithe, and when tirosh is used with dagan and yitzhar in this connection it is more properly understood to mean the produce of the vine or vintage fruit. This is especially so in this verse for the prophet is dealing with something that is eaten. Isa. 62:8,9 is the only reference of the 37 given by Burns which speaks of tirosh being something to drink and I have shown that this same passage speaks of gathering and bringing together the corn and wine (dagan and tirosh). With this one exception, yayin is the word throughout the Old Testament when wine is mentioned as something to drink, either fermented or unfermented. Of course other Hebrew words are used in this sense but the word used more than all others put together is yayin. That tirosh here in Deut. 12:7 is the fruit of the vine is clear because it is something to be eaten.

In Hosea 4:11 we read, "Whoredom and wine (yayin) and new wine (tirosh) take away the heart." This verse is used by those who hold the one wine theory that tirosh does not always mean unfermented wine because of its association here with whoredom and taking away the heart. But its use here with yayin proves too much. The One Wine Theorists also maintain that yayin always means fermented wine. That would make the verse to read, "Whoredom and fermented wine and fermented wine take away the heart." If yayin here means fermented wine, then the new wine (tirosh) would have to mean something else.

The word new here is not in the Hebrew text. The word rendered new wine is tirosh. The translators supplied the word new because they knew that tirosh is never fermented. They did this to distinguish tirosh from yayin. It should be noticed that the verse does not say that new wine takes away the heart. It says, "Whoredom and wine (yayin) and new wine (tirosh) take away the heart." By itself fresh grape juice, new wine (tirosh) does not take away the heart, and it is not conducive to evil. But when associated with whoredom it takes away the heart.

The same prophet in the preceding chapter used a similar expression in regard to pressed cakes of raisins. "Then said the Lord unto me, Go yet, love a woman beloved of her friend, yet an adulteress, according to the love of the Lord toward the children of Israel, who look to other gods, and love flagons of wine (ashishah enab, pressed cakes of raisins)" (Hos. 3:1). In dealing with the words ashishah and enab it will be seen that flagons of wine here is definitely a wrong rendering and should be pressed cakes of raisins. There is nothing evil in the use of raisins or pressed raisin cakes in themselves, but when used in the idolatrous worship of other gods they become evil because of the manner of usage.

The same is true of tirosh. By itself tirosh is not evil or conducive to evil. But when used in connection with whoredom it takes away the heart. The same could be said of orange juice or buttermilk. Of themselves they do not take away the heart. If orange juice or buttermilk were used in the idolatrous worship of other gods, they would conduce to evil because of the manner in which they were used, and in that usage it could be said, "Whoredom and orange juice take away the heart."

It should be noted here that whoredom and adultery at times in the Bible mean idolatry. Webster's Collegiate Dictionary defines whoredom as: "1. The practice of harlotry. 2. Idolatry or unfaithfulness to God, hence sinful desire." Funk & Wagnalls Standard College Dictionary: "1. The practice of illicit sexual intercourse, prostitution. 2. In the Bible, idolatry." In the fourth chapter, Hosea is speaking of idolatry when he says: "Whoredom and wine and new wine take away the heart." In Hos. 3:1, it was the use of cakes of raisins in looking to other gods that rendered them evil, and in Hos. 4:11, it was the use of tirosh along with whoredom (idolatry) that took the hearts of Israel away from the true God.

In all the scriptures where tirosh is found, not once is it spoken of as evil or conducive to evil when used by itself, or with corn and oil. It is only spoken of as evil or conducive to evil in one text where it is used in idolatrous worship (whoredom). If whoredom here is also applied to prostitution, then associating tirosh with it would render tirosh evil. The good becomes bad when it is used in connection with or to promote that which is bad.

From the foregoing testimony of Hebrew Scholars, and the use of tirosh in the Scriptures, it is this writer's firm conviction that tirosh is never fermented. If it becomes fermented it is no longer tirosh.

Chapter 5

SHEKAR — SUGAR, HONEY, AND CIDER

Shekar, (also shakar, shechar, shay-kawr) is a generic word the least understood of all the Hebrew and Greek words dealing with our subject.

Deut. 14:26, "And thou shalt bestow that money for whatsoever thy soul lusteth after, for oxen, or for sheep, or for wine (yayin), or for strong drink (shekar), or for whatsoever thy soul desireth." Giving strong drink as the meaning of shekar in this verse and in other texts where the word is used is one of the worst translational errors that we have in our English versions.

Shekar is the word from which our English word sugar derives. It is the word from which our English word cider derives. It denotes the sap taken from the trunk of the palm tree as we take the sap from the Maple tree. It denotes the thick syrup, or honey, made by boiling the palm tree sap. It denotes the sugar made from the palm syrup. It denotes a beverage enjoyed for thousands of years by Asiatics and Africans, called palm wine by some, but which is the unfermented sap of the palm tree. It denotes the juice, fermented or unfermented, from fruits other than what grows on the vine. It is the word for an intoxicating drink produced by permitting the palm sap to ferment, and its use in this form is forbidden and associated with evil in the Bible.

As used in the Bible at times, it has no intoxicating significance at all, but is erroneously rendered strong drink. Many sincere and unsuspecting church people have been led to believe that the Bible sanctions the use of such drinks as whiskey, rum, gin, brandy, vodka and other high percentage alcoholic beverages because of this translational error. I concede that in some texts shekar does mean a fermented sap or fruit juice, but certainly not every time, and never a distilled liquor.

There is an abundance of evidence that our English word sugar is but a variant or derivative of shekar.

The Popular and Critical Bible Encyclopedia says, "Shay-kawr, lucious, saccharine drink or sweet syrup, especially sugar or honey of dates or of the palm-tree (debash); also, by accommodation, occasionally, the sweet fruit itself. In Solomon's time and afterwards, says Dr. Harris, 'the wine and sweet cordials seem generally to have been used separately' (Nat. Hist. of Bible). It seems more probable, however, that the palm syrup or honey denoted by shay-kawr, was used both as a sweetmeat or article of food, and as a drink, like the Hebrew sobhe and the Roman sapa (boiled wine), diluted with water, as with the modern grape and honey syrups or sherbets (Prov. ix:2, 5). The derivative of shechar, expressive of its first signification, are numerous. Eastward and southward, following the Arabian channel and the Saracenic conquests, we meet with the most obvious forms of the

25

Hebrew word still expressive of sugar. Thus we have the Arabic sakar; Persic and Bengali, shukkur (whence our word for sugar-candy, shukur-kund, 'rock-sugar'); common Indian jagree or zhaggery; Moresque sekkour; Spanish, azucor; and Portugese assucar (molasses being mel-de-assucar 'honey of sugar,' abbreviated). The wave of population has also carried the original sense and form northwards, embodying the word in the Grecian and Teutonic languages. Hence Greek, sakehar; Latin, saccharum; Italian, zucchero; German, sucher and juderig; Dutch suiker; Russian, sachar; Danish, sukker; Swedish, socker; Welsh, siwgwr; French, sucre; and our own common words sukkar (sweetmeats), sugar, and saccharine. 'Sukkarde' is also an old English word clearly traceable in sense and sound to the same origin, and is used by the writers of the middle ages in the sense of dainty, dessert or sweetmeat."

Webster's New International Dictionary, 1959 Edition, gives the following variants for sugar: Middle English suger, sugre, sucre; Old French, sucre, sukere; French, sucre; Medieval Latin, succarum, zugurum; Arabic, sukkar; Persian, shakar, Prakrit, sakkara; Sanskrit, sarkara.

Funk & Wagnalls New Standard Dictionary, 1960 Edition gives the word for sugar in five languages: French, sucre; Late Latin, succarum; Greek, sakchar; Arabic, sakkar; Persian, shakar.

The New American Encyclopedic Dictionary, 1906 Edition, vol. v, gives three obsolete spellings for sugar: sucre, suger, and sugre; and then the following variants: French, sucre; Spanish, azucar; Arabic, sakkar, sokkar; Persian, shakar; Sanscrit, carkara; Latin, sacchurum; Greek, sakchar, sakcharon; Portugese, azucar; Italian, zucchero.

Martand Rajnoor, of India, a friend of this writer, president of a Bible college, and who has founded 24 native churches, states that in the Marathi language the word is sakhar which is identical with the Persian shakar, Arabic sakkar, and the Hebrew shekar, or shakar.

There is no doubt that our English sugar is a variant of the Hebrew shekar, and the sweet granulated article of food we use for sweetening is one of the meanings of shekar.

The word is even found in the botanical name of one of the maple trees we tap for making maple sugar. The pamphlet published by the Vermont Department of Agriculture entitled "Vermont Maple Sugar and Syrup," says, "Best for sugar making are the sugar maple, known as Acer saccharum, and the black maple."

The New American Encyclopedic Dictionary, under article Maple-sugar, says, "Chemically: Maple saccharose. A coarse sugar used by the inhabitants of the Western States of this country, obtained from the sugar-maple (Acer saccharinum)." Here again we find this ancient word in modern usage.

Our sugar substitute saccharine, which we use on the table to sweeten our coffee and tea, is also a variant of the Hebrew word. We use it in either solid or liquid form just as shekar in Bible times was either solid or liquid.

The English word we use to convert something into sugar is saccharize or saccharify. Saccharometry is the process of determining the amount of sugar in sweet solutions. All of these words are variants of the ancient shekar rendered strong drink by the translators, but which in none of the above instances means anything that is fermented or intoxicating.

The Oxford English Dictionary, Vol. 5, P. 545, gives the following definition of Jaggery, "Indo-Portugese jagara, jagra, jagre, ad. Canarese sharkare, Urdu shakkar, Sanscrit carkara: see Sugar." It next defines jaggery as, "A course dark brown sugar made in India by evaporation from the sap of various kinds of palm." Then an instance of this palm sugar being put in bags for handling, is mentioned, giving the name of the man who witnessed it in 1899, F.F. Bullen, and recorded it in the Log of the Sea Wolf. He called it jaggery, or palm sugar.

Here is identification by one of the world's most authoritative dictionaries of shekar as sugar made by boiling down the palm sap.

An ancient Israelite, speaking of sugar made by cooking palm sap would call it shekar.

Collier's Encyclopedia, Vol. 19, P. 468 says that sugar or honey is made from the sap of the palm tree and wine is made by letting the sap ferment. It identifies a particular variety of the palm tree as Jubaea spectabilis, a native of Chile which is often planted in California but does not thrive in Florida. Its distinguishing feature is its columnar trunk with a diameter of four to six feet. Notice that Collier's says that sugar and honey both are made from the palm sap.

The National Geographic, in its April 1966 issue, P. 471, gives a picture of a native of Ceylon crossing a taut ropeway stretched between two tall coconut palms as he gathers the sap which is drunk by the Ceylonese. A large pot is shown in the picture hanging by a rope from the top of one of the trees. The ancient Israelites called this shekar whether it was drunk fresh or permitted to ferment making it intoxicating. The Ceylonese now call it toddy, and the man in the picture is called a toddy tapper. The National Geographic in October 1970 carried an article telling about tapping the palm tree in India for its sap.

Again in March 1971 The National Geographic carried a 25 page report on Burma by W.E. Garrett, the Assistant Editor. On pages 344 and 345 is a colored picture of a train of oxcarts laden with large baskets of palm sugar. This cargo was being taken to a landing on the Irrawaddy River, Rudyard Kipling's Road to Mandalay. The writer tells how the juice of the toddy palm is taken from the tree like the sap from the maple tree in this country, and how it is cooked down to a delicious candy like sugar called jaggery. In Hebrew it would be called shekar. The article tells how the toddy tapper takes the sap from the tree, and how one tree will yield 120 pounds of sap a year. Not all the toddy juice is made into sugar. It can be drunk fresh, or yeast may be added so that the juice which is collected at eight o'clock in the morning will have fermented by five in the evening. By midnight it will have turned sour. The author also tells of being treated to pickled tea leaves, fried garlic, toasted sesame seeds, fried beans, and palm candy.

On page 360 is another picture of a man named Ko Than hwe climbing a palm tree to tap it for the toddy juice (jaggery — shakar, shekar). On the next page is a picture of his wife, Ma Aye Myint, boiling the sap until it thickens and crystallizes when she will shape it into golf-ball-size lumps.

I have talked with missionaries who have witnessed the natives in Asia and Africa drinking the sap obtained from the palm tree.

The Random House Dictionary of the English Language, Unabridged Edition of 1966, confirms our position that the modern word jaggery derives from the ancient shekar by defining jaggery as a coarse, dark sugar that is made from the sap of East Indian palm trees, and gives its second definition of toddy as drawn sap, esp. when fermented, of any of several toddy palms and says that toddy is a variant of tarri which is identified with the Hindi tari palmyra or palm juice.

Our position is also confirmed by The New Century Dictionary of the English Language, 1927 Edition, which shows that jaggery is a variant of the Portugese jagara, Sanskrit carkara, Prakrit sakkara, and defines it as coarse sugar made in the East Indies from the sap of palm trees, and gives the same definition for palm sugar.

Webster's Third International Dictionary, 1961 Edition says that jaggery, also jagghery and jaggary, is the Hindi tari juice of the palyra palm and gives the definition as the fresh or unfermented sap of various East Indian palm, and gives the definition of palm wine as the fermented sap of any of various palms used as a beverage esp. in tropical countries. This latter definition is not sufficient for the palm wine is used as a beverage before fermentation as well as after.

I have already given the Oxford Dictionary definition of jaggery, but it might be well to note that the Oxford Dictionary also gives other spellings of the same word as gagara, jagra, jeggery, jagre, jaggaree, jaggory, jagree, jagory, jagery, jaggeree, jaggare, jahhery, jahhari.

Oxford's definition of toddy is a sap obtained from various species of palm and used as a beverage in tropical countries, and adds that it is also the intoxicating liquor by its fermentation.

Before closing this chapter, we need to look at one more word that is derived from shekar. That is the word cider. The New American Encyclopedic Dictionary gives five spellings of the word, four of which are now archaic: cider, cyder, cyser, sydir, sidir, then the word's equivalent in other languages is give: Latin, sicera; Greek, sikera; French, cidre; Spanish, sidra; Portugese, cidra; and adds that cider comes from the Hebrew shekar.

Funk & Wagnalls Standard Family Dictionary defines cider as the expressed juice of apples used as a beverage before and after fermentation, and then gives the old English form as sidre, the Late Latin as sicera, and says that cider comes from the Hebrew shekar.

Funk & Wagnalls Desk Standard Dictionary also shows that the word cider comes from the Hebrew Shekar.

The New Testament Greek equivalent of the Hebrew shekar is sikera, occuring only in Luke 1:15. The angel told Zacharias that his son, John the Baptist should not drink wine or strong drink. The Greek word for strong drink here is sikera. The Hebrew shekar appears 22 times in the Old Testament. In our King James Version it is rendered strong drink 21 times and strong wine once. The Septuagint Greek Version of the Old Testament uses the word sikera 12 times in translating the Hebrew shekar.

When Wycliff was translating the Greek New Testament into English, for Luke 1:15, "He shall be great in the sight of the Lord, and shall drink neither wine (oinon) nor strong drink (sikera), he wrote, "He schal not drynke wyn and sydir," a rendering much more proper than strong drink.

Here is Biblical proof that our English word cider is cognate with both the Hebrew shekar and the Greek sikera.

Many language scholars have been impressed with the similarity of the Hebrew and English tongues. William Tyndale, who translated the Bible into English in 1525, mentioned this similarity. In 1528 Tyndale published a book titled "Obedience of a Christian Man," in which he answered those who criticised him for translating the Bible on the grounds that the English language was not capable of a proper translation. A copy of his book can be found in the British Museum. J. Courteney James, on the fly leaf of his book "Hebrew and English Some Likenesses Psychic and Linguistic," by permission of the British Museum, has reproduced a photo of a page of Tyndale's book which has this statement: "Why then mighte they not be writte in the mother tonge. As yf one of us preach a good sermon why maye it not be written? Gaynt hierom also translated the bible in to his mother tonge. Why maye not we also? They will saye it can not be translated in to oure tonge it is so rude. It is not so rude as theyu are false lyers. For the Greke tonge agreeth moare with the english than with the latyne. And the *properties of the hebrue tonge agreeth a thousand tymes moare with the english then with the latyne." He then goes on and argues for a direct translation from the Hebrew into English, rather than from Hebrew into Latin, and then from Latin into English.

I give this from Tyndale for the purpose of showing the similarity of Hebrew and English words. This is particularly so with shekar. Both of our English words sugar and cider come from shekar and the Hebrew word conveys the same meaning as its English cognates. This similarity of English and Hebrew is also seen in our word wine which is cognate with the Hebrew yain, pronounced as yah-een, similar to the sound of the English wine.

Wycliff also was apparently impressed with this similarity and this accounts for his use of cider as the English cognate for the Greek sikera and the Hebrew shekar. If other translators had seen the similarity of these English, Hebrew and Greek words we would not have as much confusion over the word shekar.

Chapter 6

SHEKAR AND PALM WINE

Few Americans or Englishmen know about tapping the palm tree and using the sap to make sugar or palm wine. Ignorance of this practice accounts for much of the difficulty the translators have had with the word shekar. When the Wycliff translation, the Tyndale translation, the Bishop's Bible, the Geneva Bible, and the King James Version were being prepared, all of them before 1611 A.D., travel was much more restricted than it is now, and knowledge of the customs of the people in Asia, Africa, and of course in the Americas was very limited. It was not known then, and is not generally known today that sugar and honey were made from the palm sap and that sap, fermented and unfermented, was also used extensively as a beverage, and called palm wine.

James Hasting's Encyclopedia of Religion and Ethics, Vol. 5, P. 73, says: "The discovery of the drink value of the sap of certain trees was not difficult. Those chiefly used are palms, sugar canes, and agaves."

The Encyclopedia then goes on to say that palm wine is the universal drink and is commonly used all over the continent of Africa. It is used in Madagascar, the East Indian Islands, Celebes and the Moluccas, in Java, Sumatra, Malaysia, India. It is called sagero in the Moluccas which identifies it with the Hebrew shakar, shekar. The article states that the people of Tenimber and Timorlaut, because of their belief that adaptation to climatic conditions is partly affected by diet, say that it is impossible to live in those islands without drinking a sufficiency of palm wine. While the writer makes no mention of the palm wine being taken in its fresh unfermented state, still the relationship of the palm wine to the Hebrew shekar is shown. The chief tree used in the Moluccas for the juice is the Arengo saccharifera. The Hebrew shakar is embodied in this name.

The Greek Historian Herodotus, called the Father of History, who lived in the fifth century B.C. gives us an idea of how ancient the practice of making palm wine was: "Palm trees grow in great numbers over the whole flat country, mostly the kind which bears fruit, and this fruit supplies them with bread, wine, and honey." Herodotus does not make it clear whether the wine and honey are made from the sap or the dates, but he does show that in the land he was writing about wine and honey were made from the palm tree, and there is an abundance of evidence from other sources that wine and honey were made from the palm tree juice or sap.

The New American Encyclopedic Dictionary, Vol. V, P. 4522, in its definition of wine shows that palm juice was called wine, and that it did not have to be fermented to be wine: "The unfermented juice of certain plants; as palm wine."

31

In addition to what it says about palm sugar, The Popular and Critical Bible Encyclopedia is quite explicit in dealing with palm wine. It says: "(2) Date or Palm Wine. Date or Palm wine in its fresh or unfermented state. Bishop Lowth translates Is. xxiv:9 thus, — 'With songs they shall no more drink wine (i.e., of grapes); The palm wine shall be bitter to them that drink it' — and observes, note in loc., that 'this is the proper meaning of the word shekar; Gr. sikera. All enjoyment shall cease; the sweetest wine shall become bitter to their taste.'"

The article then quotes from The Mohammedan Travel (A.D. 850) who says that "palm wine, if drunk fresh, is sweet like honey; but if kept, it turns to vinegar."

A quotation from Mandelsloh, 1640 A.D., who wrote in Ambassador's Travels about the village of Demre near Surat, is given: "Terry or Palm Wine. In this village we found some terry, which is a liquor drawn out of the palm trees, they go up to the top of the tree, where they make an incision in the bark, and fasten under it an earthen pot, which they leave there all night, in which time it is filled with a certain sweet liquor very pleasant to the taste. They get out some also in the daytime, but that (owing to the great heat) corrupts immediately, and is good only for vinegar, which is all the use they make of it."

Then from an Italian writer, Adam Fabroni, who says that "the palm trees, which particularly abounded in the vicinity of Jericho and Engaddi, also served to make a very sweet wine, which is made all over the East being called palm wine by the Latins, and syra in India, from the Persian shir, which means luscious liquor or drink" (On the Husbandry of the Ancient Jews).

A quotation from Dr. Shaw is given about unfermented palm wine: "This liquor, which has a more luscious sweetness than honey, is of the consistence of a thin syrup, but quickly grows tart and ropy acquiring an intoxicating quality."

Then follows the last quotation we shall make from this Encyclopedia. It gives a statement from Sir G.T. Temple's Expediation to the Niger: "We were daily supplied with the sap of the date-tree, which is a delicious and wholesome beverage when drunk quite fresh; but if allowed to remain for some hours, it acquires a sharp taste, not unlike cider . . . The landers inform us that 'palm wine is the common and favorite drink of the natives' of Africa — that the juice is called wine and that 'it is either used in this state, or preserved till it acquires rather a bitter flavor.'"

Encyclopedia Britannica shows that both wine and sugar are among the products obtained from the palm tree and lists seventeen specific articles that it furnishes.

Encyclopedia Americana says that toddy, arrach, jaggery and vinegar are produced from the juice of the palm tree and says that the kittul or toddy palm Caryota urens of India and Malaya is "most noted for its production of toddy, or palm wine; a good tree yields amounts to 25 quarts a day per tree."

Dr. Lees says, "Shakar, erroneously translated strong drink, comes from an Oriental root for 'sweet-juice,' and is the undoubted original of the

32

European words (Greek, Latin, Teutonic, and Spanish) for sugar. It is used to this day in Arabia for palm-juice and palm-wine, whether fresh or fermented. In the Common Version of the Bible, there is just one text, and only one, that gives apparent Divine sanction to intoxicating wine, namely Deut. 14:26, where strong drink is named as a permissible element in a sacred feast. The answer is conclusive, — no word for 'strong' exists in the Hebrew text. The term there used is simply SHAKAR, — the original of saccar, sugar. It denoted Palm Wine in various states, unfermented, sweet, and syrupy, as well as intoxicating and 'bitter.' Hence, as Bishop Lowth observes, the antitheses of Isaiah, — 'Thy shechar (sweet wine) shall become bitter,' — i.e., deteriorated, which it does when fermented."

Burns similarly says, "Shakar, translated in our version 'strong drink' and once (Numbers xxviii. 7) 'strong wine,' is the venerable lingual ancester of our familiar 'sugar,' and especially denotes the sweet juice of other fruits than the grape, also the juice of the palm tree. Sweetness, not alcoholic strength, was its characteristic; hence the point of the threatening (Is. xxiv. 9), that it should become 'bitter' to those who drink it. Nothing is more common in the East, at the present day, than for the palm-juice to be drunk in its fresh and noninebriating state. No doubt yayin and shakar were often allowed to ferment, and used in that state, and were also frequently mixed with drugs, to increase their intoxicating potency; but whenever they are named in Scripture, in language implying Divine approbation, there is either a direct or tacit reference to them as natural bounties, the offspring of vital growth, and no word is ever employed of them as fermented liquors."

We have been considering shekar in its liquid form known as palm wine or toddy, both fermented and unfermented. There is still another form of palm sap which is of a higher alcoholic content than is produced by fermentation alone. That is arrack, which is the palm sap first fermented, then distilled. Funk & Wagnalls Desk Standard Dictionary defines arrack: "A strong oriental liquor distilled from the juice of the coco-palm, etc. hence any distilled liquor."

Arrack is not the same as American corn whiskey. Neither is the hot toddy we make with whiskey, sugar and hot water the same as the toddy of the Orient, which is palm sap.

Webster's Third International Dictionary defines arrach thus: "Arrack, also arak, or arrak (Arabic araq sweet juice, liquor): an alcoholic beverage from the Far East or Near East: esp. a liquor of high alcoholic content resembling rum in taste and distilled in the Far East from fermented juice of the coconut palm or from a fermented mash or rice or molasses."

With modern distillation the fermented juice of the palm is made into a much stronger alcoholic drink than was developed in ancient times by mere fermentation. However, distillation was a process unknown to the ancient Israelites, and while palm wine (shekar), both unfermented and fermented, was known to them, distilled palm wine or arrach was not known.

I have already mentioned Oxford's definition of jaggery and toddy. In its definition of palm sugar, Oxford Dictionary says it is "the sugar produced from the palm sap," and palm wine is "wine made from the sap of the palm tree." The article on palm wine then goes on to quote from a traveller in 1866 who wrote, "Palm toddy is intoxicating, and when distilled yields strong arrack . . . but its most important product is jaggery, or palm sugar." Then a quotation from the missionary Livingstone, 1857. Trav. xxi, 411, "The men. . . spend most of their time in drinking palm toddy. This toddy is the juice of the palm-oil tree . . . a sweet clear liquid not at all intoxicating while fresh, but when allowed to stand till the afternoon, causes inebriation."

The World Book Encyclopedia, 1964 Edition confirms what has been given above: "The sugary sap of such palms as the jaggery can be made into food, sweet drinks, and intoxicating beverages such as arrack."

The 9th Edition of Britannica, on the subject of Dates, gives four different products of palm sap: the juice boiled down into sugar (shekar), the fresh juice in its original unfermented state (shekar), the fermented juice (shekar), and the fermented juice distilled to make arrack.

Funk & Wagnalls Encyclopedia, 1952 Edition, P. 9306, gives its support to what I have given in this chapter saying that the sap of the jaggery palm (shekar) is sweet and furnishes palm sugar (shekar), that the sap is used as a beverage (shekar), which is sometimes fermented to make palm wine. All those who enjoy drinking the juice pressed from the apple at harvest time know that it is called cider in its fresh and unfermented state. If permitted to set for a time it ferments and becomes intoxicating, but it is still called cider. To distinguish between the unfermented and the fermented, the first is called sweet cider and the latter hard cider. Similarly the sap from the palm tree is called palm wine whether fermented or unfermented, and the word shekar is used for both.

From what has been given in these two chapters from Encyclopedias, Dictionaries, and writers, whose scholarship has earned them the right to speak, the Hebrew word shekar is established beyond reasonable doubt to mean the sap of the palm tree in its different forms: unfermented, syrup, honey, sugar, sweet cider, hard cider, fermented palm sap, etc. The fermented palm sap is now distilled and called arrack, which has a much higher alcoholic content, but arrack was not known to the ancient Israelites, and the word arrack is not cognate with shekar.

Chapter 7

THE USE OF SHEKAR SANCTIONED AND CONDEMNED

In the Bible, the use of shekar is both sanctioned and condemned. This leaves the Bible student in a quandary if the word always means strong drink and nothing else. But I have shown in the two preceding chapters that this rendering is not proper. I have shown that shekar is a generic term and fermented palm wine is merely one of its several meanings. I have given the testimony of men whose scholarship cannot be questioned. I have quoted from dictionaries and encyclopedias that are recognized authorities. If the reader feels that I have been too lengthy in my dealing with this word, I reply that the only way of correcting the long-standing but erroneous concept of shekar as being always and only a fermented or even distilled drink of high alcoholic content is by showing that the overwhelming weight of scholarship is against it.

The King James Translators, and other translators, had a word that was the English equivalent for the Hebrew yain, and they used the word wine. They had two English words that were cognates for shekar, which were cider and sugar, but they used the words strong drink, which is not a translation at all, the Hebrew word for strong not once being used in any connection with shekar, and one of the meanings of the word is sugar which is not a drink but a granulated sweetener used for sweetening other foods.

There is no justification for using the word strong, and this has been partly responsible for the confusion on this subject. It would have been better if the word shekar had not been translated at all, but given in its original Hebrew form. In another chapter we shall consider the term strong drink more fully.

With the information in the preceding chapters, it is no longer difficult to arrive at the true meaning of Deut. 14:26: "And thou shalt bestow that money for whatsoever thy soul lusteth after, for oxen, or for sheep, or for wine (yain), or for strong drink (shekar), or for whatsoever thy soul desireth."

I have shown that yain, yayin, is a generic word for grapes, raisins, unfermented grape juice, grape syrup, grape jam, and also fermented grape juice. I have also shown that shekar is a generic word for sugar, syrup or honey made from palm sap, the sweet unfermented sap of the palm tree, the fermented palm sap, and cider either sweet or fermented.

In view of all the condemnation pronounced upon the one who is deceived by, uses, or gives fermented wine to his neighbor; and in view of the fact that the use of such things are prohibited especially to the Nazarites, kings, and priests; and in view of the fact that Deut. 14:26 is given in connection with a special religious gathering at Jerusalem in which the king, the priests, and the Nazarites would all take part; it is contrary to all the general teaching of the Word of God to even assume that the Lord would instruct Israel to use intoxicating drinks in a religious celebration. To say that yain and shekar here mean fermented wine and drink of a high alcoholic content renders the Bible self-contradictory and robs it of its infallibility. It is clear that the two words here mean the produce of the vine and of the palm tree which are not alcoholic.

Cider, Sugar, unfermented palm juice, palm honey, sugar syrup are all products that would be included in the use of shekar, even rock candy made from the palm sugar, but not fermented palm wine. All products of the grape vine are included in Deut. 14:26 with the exception of the fermented grape juice. To take any other position and use this verse as a justification for taking fermented grape wine or palm wine on this religious occasion contradicts all other texts where the use of such things as prohibited. God cannot contradict Himself.

It is admitted that in some texts shekar does mean a fermented drink, but never does it mean a distilled drink with high alcoholic content, and in other passages it has no significance of anything fermented. It cannot mean a strong drink such as whiskey, gin, rum, vodka, etc., for distillation was unknown to the Israelites.

I repeat that nowhere in the Bible are the Hebrew or Greek words meaning strong used in any connection with shekar or sikera. This has been a tragic blunder on the part of the translators.

Chapter 8

ENAB — WINE OR GRAPES?

Flagons of wine or pressed cakes of raisins. Which should it be? In the King James Version the expression flagons of wine appears three times, and the word flagons without the word wine is found once. This is quite different to what the Hebrew text actually says. The words rendered flagons and wine in the English version are ashishah and enab. Only once in the four times that ashishah appears in the Hebrew text is it accompanied with the word enab.

It is apparent that the translators were not certain about their rendering of flagons of wine. This is clearly seen by their use of italics and marginal reading.

2 Sam. 6:19, "And he dealt among all the people, even among the whole multitude of Israel, as well to the women as men, to every one a cake of bread, and a good piece of flesh, and a flagon of wine." The words "of flesh" and "of wine" are in italics to indicate that they were not in the Hebrew text, and the translators supplied them in an effort to make the meaning more complete. This is an unfortunate rendering.

1 Chron. 16:3, "And he dealt to every one of Israel, both man and women, to every one a loaf of bread, and a good piece of flesh, and a flagon of wine." Again the words "of wine" are in italics, indicating that the translators supplied them but they were not in the Hebrew text.

Songs of Sol. 2:5, "Stay me with flagons, comfort me with apples: for I am sick of love." Here the words "of wine" are absent and flagons is used by itself.

Hos. 3:1, " . . . who look to other gods, and love flagons of wine." This is the only one of the four verses where flagons is found that the word enab, rendered wine by the translators, appears in the Hebrew. But even here the translators apparently were not certain for in the margin they gave an alternate reading, "of grapes," and this is the proper rendering.

In all of the other 18 texts where the word enab appears, the translators have rightly rendered it grapes 17 times, and ripe grapes once.

Davies' Complete Hebrew and Chaldee Lexicon, founded on the works of Gesenius and Furst, defines enab as "m. Prop. what is round or globular, a berry, esp. a grape." Then he cites Deut. 32:14, "the blood of the grape (enab);" Num. 13:23, "one cluster of grapes (enab);" and Gen. 40:10, "the clusters thereof brought forth ripe grapes (enab);" also Gen. 49:11, "he washed his garments in wine (yayin), and his clothes in the blood of grapes (enab)."

37

Young defines the word as "A (ripe or round) grape, grape cake." When consulting Strong's Hebrew and Chaldee Dictionary, and his Greek Dictionary, in the back of his Concordance, the reader should keep in mind that Strong follows a pattern in giving definitions, which is explained at the beginning of the dictionary under "Plan of the Book." First the appropriate number of the word is given, then the Hebrew, Chaldee or Greek word in its original letters. Next is given the equivalent English letters followed by the proper pronunciation. Then the etymology, radical meaning, and applied significance, or definition, is given. Finally, the colon and dash (:-) punctuation marks are given, after which are the different renderings of the word in the King James Version, some of which may not be in keeping with Strong's definition at times. For instance, enab is defined by Strong as a grape, but he shows that it is rendered (ripe) grape and also wine in the King James Version. But wine is not Strong's definition.

Ben-Yehuda's Hebrew Dictionary for the English word grape gives enab, but does not give enab for the word wine. The Companion Bible, with no sympathy for our unfermented wine position, admits that flagons of wine should be rendered cakes of grapes in Hos. 3:1.

A modern confirmation of our position that enab means grapes is given by Mary Hughes, writing in the Sept. 1970 issue of Kingdom Digest about how the British Army freed Jerusalem from the Turks in 1917. She tells how "the 180th Brigade moved on toward Kuryet el enab, which translated means, 'the hill of grapes.'"

Not only does enab mean grapes but it also is used in the Bible for raisins, dried grapes. Num 6:3, "He shall separate himself from wine (yayin) and strong drink (shekar), and shall drink no vinegar (chomets) of wine (yayin), or vinegar (chomets) of strong drink (shekar), neither shll he drink any liquor (mishrah) of grapes (enab), nor eat moist grapes (enab) or dried." Some translations say, "fresh grapes or dried."

I have shown that the word wine is cognate with yain which includes grapes as one of its several meanings and therefore wine in an extended meaning also includes grapes. It would hardly be acceptable though for the translators to render the passage in Hos. 3:1, "who look to other gods, and love cakes (ashishah) of wine (enab). But the common rendering "flagons (jugs or bottles) of wine" is less acceptable for ashishah definitely does not mean a bottle or jug; it means cakes and the passage should read "cakes of raisins or dried grapes (enab)," as we shall see in the next chapter in our study on the word ashishah.

Chapter 9

ASHISHAH, FLAGONS OF WINE OR
CAKES OF RAISINS, WHICH?

In the King James Version, ashishah is rendered flagons. Funk & Wagnalls Standard College Dictionary says that a flagon is, "A vessel with a handle and a spout, and often a hinged lid, used to serve liquids. A large wine bottle." The word derives from Old French flacon, flascon, and Medieval Latin flasco. Our word flask is a variant of flagon.

In the preceding I gave the four texts in which the word flagons (ashishah) appears. I also stated that flagons is an improper rendering of ashishah. Every Hebrew scholar I have consulted shows that this is a wrong translation and the word should be rendered cake of raisins, cake of dried grapes, or a similar expression, but not a liquor of any kind.

Strong defines the word as something that is closely pressed together, such as a cake of raisins or other comfits. Young says a cake of grapes. Burns says, "Ashishah is admitted by all writers to refer, not to wine, but to pressed cakes of grapes." Douglas writes, "But by universal consent it is now understood to be some kind of cake — probably a cake of dried fruit; perhaps of dried grapes, as there is another term for a cake of figs." Dr. Lees says a fruit-cake. Fausset says it should be translated grape cakes. Samson, "The word ashishah rendered 'flagon,' used four times, refers doubtless to dried grapes and raisins pressed into cakes," and adds that Fuerst thus interprets it and cites as authority both the Sept. Greek Translation and the Talmud. Davies' Lexicon says, "Cake, prop. something pressed together, hence raisin — Cakes."

The following translations confirm this rendering. Moffatt says, "a bunch of raisins" in 2 Sam. 6:19, and 1 Chron. 16:3; "raisins" in Cant. 2:5; and "raisin-cakes" in Hos. 3:1. Rotherham says, "a raisin cake" in 2 Sam. 6:19 and 1 Chron. 16:3; and "raisin cakes" in Cant. 2:5 and Hos. 3:1. The American Standard Version and English Revised Version both say, "a cake of raisins" in 2 Sam. 6:19 and 1 Chron. 16:3; "raisins" in Cant. 2:5, giving "cakes of raisins" in the footnote; and "cakes of raisins" in Hos. 3:1. The Revised Standard Version says, "a cake of raisins" in 2 Sam. 6:19, and 1 Chron. 16:3; "raisins" in Cant. 2:5; and "cakes of raisins" in Hos. 3:1. Young's Literal Translation leaves 2 Sam. 6:19 untranslated, saying "and one ashisha:" but gives "a grape cake" in 1 Chron. 16:3; and grape-cakes" in both Cant. 2:5 and Hos. 3:1.

From the above, it is quite apparent that flagons of wine is an unjustifiable rendering of ashishah. The One Wine Theorists have used the King James rendering of these verses in their arguing that the Bible sanctions

39

the use of fermented wine, but a proper understanding of the meaning of the word ashishah and the word enab completely undermines their position.

Chapter 10

ASIS, FRESH GRAPE JUICE

Asis (also given as aciyc, ahsis, ausees) appears five times in the Old Testament Hebrew. Once it is rendered juice; twice it is rendered sweet wine; and twice new wine in our King James Version.

Rendering this word sweet wine and new wine furnishes us with the strongest proof that our English word wine means the fresh and unfermented grape juice as well as the fermented, for asis always means the sweet and unfermented juice of the grape.

Samson says, "The term asis, used five times, rendered 'sweet wine' (Isa. 49:26, and Amos 9:13), 'new wine' (Joel 1:5, and 3:16), and 'juice' (Cant. 8:2), derived from asas meaning to 'press,' indicates the fresh juice oozing from the fruit" (Cycl. of Temp. & Pro.).

Ben-Yehuda's Pocket English Hebrew Dictionary gives asis as the Hebrew for juice.

Faussett says, "Asis, from a root to 'tread,' the grape juice newly expressed (S. of Sol. viii.2); 'sweet wine' (Isa. xlix. 26, Amos ix. 13); 'new wine' (Joel 1. 5, iii. 18)."

Davies says, "Asis m. prop. trodden out i.e. from grapes (r. asas), hence new wine or must (L. mustum) Joel 1, 5, Am. 9, 13, prob. intoxicating Is. 49, 26; made also from pomegranates Can. 8, 2." While Davies fell into the common error of assuming that the language of Is. 49:26 calls for an intoxicating wine, which will be considered later, he still recognized that the proper meaning of asis was freshly trodden out wine or must, which comes from the Latin mustum and means freshly expressed grape juice.

The use of asis in Amos 9:13 clearly shows that fresh or new wine, unfermented juice is indicated, "Behold, the days come, saith the Lord, that the plowman shall overtake the reaper, and the treader of grapes (enab) him that soweth seed; and the mountains shall drop sweet wine (asis), and all the hills shall melt." "The mountains shall drop sweet wine." This is a figure of speech describing conditions that will obtain when the Lord pours out his blessings on restored Israel. The vineyards on the mountain side shall bear such vintage that before the harvesters can gather it in the ripe grapes will begin to burst their skins and the sweet wine (asis) will drop from the clusters.

For sweet wine (asis) the Septuagint Greek Version has the word glukasmon in this verse. Burns tells us that this word means sweetness, which is the meaning of the Latin word given in the Latin Vulgate Version for this reference.

The entire passage, verses 11 to 15, deal with restored Israel. The language is metaphoric, for mountains of themselves do not drop with either sweet wine or fermented wine. But grapes do burst forth and the sweet unfermented juice does drop from them if not gathered soon enough. The use of any word here denoting an intoxicating or fermented wine would be entirely out of place. The Hebrew, Septuagint Greek, and Latin Vulgate all use words that indicate a fresh juice that is not fermented.

Joel 3:18 uses the same expression, "the mountains shall drop down new wine (asis)," describing millenial conditions, and again the Septuagint Greek word is glukasmon, from which we get our English glucose.

Joel 1:5 uses the word asis along with yayin. "Awake, ye drunkards, and weep; and howl, all ye drinkers of wine (yayin), because of the new wine (asis); for it is cut off from your mouth." Two kinds of wine are mentioned in this verse, but it needs to be studied in its full context.

The entire chapter is an exhortation to mourning, "For a nation is come upon my land, strong, and without number, ... He hath laid my vine waste, ... and the new wine (tirosh) is dried up, the oil languisheth ... The vine is dried up, and the fig tree languisheth; the pomegranite tree, the palm tree also, and the apple tree, even all the trees of the field, are withered" (verses 6-12). Verse 4 describes the blight caused by the palmerworm, locust, cankerworm, and caterpiller even before the invasion by the enemy nation. As a result of all this devastation there would be no figs, grapes, pomegranates, dates, apples, no more tirosh (fruit of the vine), asis (fresh juice of the fruit), or yayin (fermented juice).

Asis not only denoted the fresh juice of the grape, but was also used for the juice of other fruits. In Cant. 8:2 it is the juice of the pomegranate. "I would cause thee to drink of spiced wine (yayin reqach) of the juice (asis) of my pomegranate (rimmon)." Asis was applied to the fresh juice of the grape, but it was also the custom to squeeze the juice from the pomegranate and this also was called both asis and yayin. At times spices were added to the fruit juices, both fermented and unfermented, to increase the flavor, and at times drugs were added to the fermented wine to increase the intoxicating effect. When this was done to either the fermented or unfermented juice it was called spiced wine (yayin reqach).

Adding of spices and aromatics to their fruit juices was similar to the modern custom of adding cinnamon and cloves to apple cider and drinking it hot. This is a delightful beverage which this writer has enjoyed many times. Of course we used sweet cider. The ancients would call it spiced wine (yayin reqach). I do not know whether they drank it hot or cold.

The last scripture in which asis appears is Isa. 49:26, "And I will feed them that oppress thee with their own flesh; and they shall be drunken with their own blood, as with sweet wine (margin says new wine): and all flesh shall know that I the Lord am thy Saviour and thy Redeemer the mighty One of Jacob." "Drunken with their own blood, as with sweet wine (asis)." This expression has been used as a proof text for showing that asis means an intoxicating wine for unfermented grape juice does not intoxicate. To which we reply neither does blood intoxicate. The entire verse is figurative.

42

The preceding verse shows that the Lord is speaking about Israel's enemies, "For I will contend with him that contendeth with thee," and if the verse is to be taken literally it would mean that the one who contended with Israel would have to eat his own flesh and drink his own blood, which would be utterly impossible.

Douglas says that this passage is no proof that must, which is unintoxicating, cannot be meant here, for neither is blood intoxicating, and all that the verb necessarily conveys is to drink till one is satiated or cloyed.

The sense of the verse is that God's judgements on those who contended with Israel would be great and terrible. If it is insisted that the verse must be taken literally and that it is proof that asis is intoxicating, then let them give one instance in history when the enemies of Israel actually ate their own flesh and became intoxicated with their own blood.

The fact that translators have rendered asis as new wine, and that lexicographers say that asis means the freshly expressed juice of the grape or other fruit, is evidence that our English word wine means unfermented juice as well as the fermented. It also shows that in Bible times unfermented juice was in common usage.

Certainly the Lord, by design, had His prophets use the word asis in these scriptures, and the use of this word upsets the wine cart of the One Wine Theorists.

Chapter 11

SOBE — GRAPE SYRUP OR DRUNKARD?

Sobe (also sobhe, sove, soveh, soba, so'beth, cobe) is the Hebrew word to which the Latin word sapa is cognate. The Latins boiled the grape juice (mustum) until it became thick, and then stored it for future use when they would mix it with water to make it thin again for drinking, or spread it on bread as we do our jellies and jams.

Sobe is found four times in the Old Testament and is rendered wine, drink, drunken, drunkard. Isa. 1:22, "Their silver is become dross, their wine (sobe) is mixed. Hos. 4:18, "Their drink (sobe) is sour." Nah. 1:10, "For while they be folden together as thorns, and while they are drunken (sobe) as drunkards (sobe), they shall be devoured as stubble fully dry."

This word has a limited use in the Bible, and none of the four times it is found will affect the outcome of this treatise, still we need to study the word because it is cognate to the Latin sapa, and it appears that the translators had a struggle with its meaning in Nah. 1:10.

Sobe appears to have had a concrete meaning and an abstract meaning. Strong says that cobe means a "potation, concretely (wine), or abstractly (carousal)." He then shows that the word is rendered drink, drunken, wine, which gives us little help. But he also states that cobe comes from caba which he defines as a primitive root meaning to quaff to satiety, i.e. become tipsy.

Young's definition is not much better, "Anything sucked in or up." The word saba, rendered drunkard and drunken, Young defines as, "to suck up, be satiated," and "to drink."

Other writers are more specific than Strong and Young. Burns says, "Soveh was a rich, thick, and probably boiled wine, greatly relished, not for any alcoholic property, being more of a jelly than a liquid."

Samson writes, "The word 'soba,' three times used (Isa. 1:22; Hos. 4:18; Nah. 1:10), rendered 'wine,' 'drink,' and 'drunken,' and described in Isa. 1:22 as mixed with water, as in Latin and other translations indicate, is a syrup made of fresh grape-juice, like those used in making effervescing drinks, and common among Mohammedans as the drink called 'sherbet'" (Cyclo. of Tem. & Pro.).

Fred C. Hitt, "So'beth, used about three times, meaning to drink freely because the heavy, thick, boiled juice was thinned with water, and could be drunk freely."

Douglas says, "Sobhe or sove is a word with which we meet only thrice, and whose meaning therefore cannot much affect the current interpretation. There is considerable probability that it is copied in the Latin word

45

sapa, 'boiled wine,' or more precisely 'must boiled down:' and when it was so far inspissated to become syrup, it might be included under the name Honey, . . . In Ho. iv. 18, 'Their drink is sour,' it might be natural to trace a contrast to the original sweetness of this inspissated wine; but the simplest translation is, 'Their sobhe is gone;' from which we are not able to learn anything of its nature. The third passage, Na. 1. 10, is obscure, and no light will probably be reflected from it on the precise meaning of this term."

While the King James Version reads, "Their drink is sour," in the main text for Hos. 4:18, the marginal reading says, "Their drink is gone." Fenton writes, "Their drink is out." Leeser, "Their drinking bout will come to an end." The Popular and Critical Bible Encyclopedia says, "It seems more probable, however, that the palm syrup or honey denoted by shay-kawr, was used both as a sweetmeat or article of food, and as a drink, like the Hebrew sobhe and the Roman sapa (boiled wine), diluted with water, as with the modern grape and honey syrups or sherbets" (Art. Drink Strong). This helps us to understand the word sobe, but gives no help on Hos. 4:18.

For Nah. 1:10 there seems to be about as many translations as there are translators. The New Catholic Bible says, "So while they are feasting and drinking together." Rotherham, "And as drunkards drenched with their drink." Leeser, "And as men made drunken in their drinking bout." Rubin, "And as men made drunken in their drinking bout." Moffatt completely omits the clause. Fenton, "And like drunkards confused in their drink." Young, "And with their drink are drunken." The Septuagint Greek makes no mention of wine, drink, drinking, drunkenness, or drunkards. Lamsa's Translation of the Aramaic, "They stagger in their drunkenness. Revised Standard Version omits the clause in the text but gives a footnote which says, "Heb. are consumed, drunken as with their drink."

It can readily be seen that there has been an uncertainty in the minds of translators about this word, but it is the same word that the King James Version renders wine in Isa. 1:22, but drunken and drunkards in Nah. 1:10.

Regardless of the difficulty this word has given translators, there is no doubt that sobe is the word from which the Latin sapa derived, and the Latin sapa was a thick syrup or paste made from boiling the grape juice (must) and was mixed with water or milk for drinking or spread on bread as we do with our jellies and jams. The use of wine (grape syrup or jam) mixed with milk or water was a common practice and nowhere is it condemned in the Word. Fermented wine mixed with drugs was condemned. It's only permissive use was as a sedative to relieve pain in one about to die, or as a merciful stupefier for one facing execution.

Chapter 12

YEQEB — WINE OR WINEPRESS?

Yeqeb (also yaqueb, yequeb), which is translated wine only once in the sixteen times it appears in the Hebrew text, is our next consideration.

Young's definition of this word is, "Press or vat for wine or oil."

Strong says, "From an unused root meaning to excavate; a trough (as dug out); spec. a wine-vat (whether the lower one, into which the juice drains; or the upper, in which the grapes are crushed)."

Fausset, in his comments on "Fat," differs slightly with Strong and says that the Hebrew gath is the upper receptacle where the grapes were trod and the yeqeb was the lower vat which the juice flowed into, but he agrees that the root meaning was to hollow for the gath (winepress) and the fat (vat) or yeqeb into which the juice flowed were both dug out of the rocks of the hills where the vineyards were (Com. Mark xxi.1, Isa. v.2 Marg).

Davies agrees with Fausset in his definition of the Hebrew gath, defining it as the wine-press or the trough in which the grapes were pressed, and from which the juice flowed into the yeqeb.

Of the sixteen times yeqeb appears in the Old Testament Hebrew, the King James Version renders it winepress 10 times; press-fat 1 time; press 2 times; fat 2 times; and wine once. It might be well to insert here that our modern English word vat was formerly spelled with an F. The Old English spelling was fat, Anglo-Saxon faet, Icelandic fat, Swedish fat.

In Deut. 16:13 the word yeqeb is rendered wine in our English Version. "Thou shalt observe the feast of tabernacles seven days, after that thou hast gathered in thy corn and thy wine (yeqeb).

The following translations render the word winepress: Rubin, Leeser, American Standard Version, Moffatt, New Catholic Bible, English Revised Version, Revised Standard Version, Lamsa, and Brenton's Septuagint Greek and English. Rotherham and Young's Literal Translation say wine-vat.

In view of the above translations and the fact that in the other fifteen times the word is translated in the King James Version as winepress, press-fat, press, fat, there should be no question about the real meaning of the word.

Why then did the King James translators use the word wine in this one instance, when it is clear that they knew the meaning of the word? They knew what most people do not know today that the freshly expressed juice of the grape was wine, and in describing the taking of the fresh grape juice (must) from the vat, they said, "after thou hast gathered in thy corn and thy wine."

Moses and the King James translators were not speaking of harvesting corn from the field or grapes from the vineyard. The margin shows this to be so. The word corn has a marginal note which says, "Heb. floor, and thy winepress." They gathered the grain off the threshing floor, and the wine, the sweet juice, the must, from the winepress.

The word corn is defined by Webster's Collegiate Dictionary, Fifth Edition, as: "Any small, hard seed; esp., the seed of any one of the cereal grasses. Collectively, the seeds of any of the cereal grasses used for food; grain. Corn in England refers to wheat, in Scotland and Ireland to oats, and in the United States and Australia to Indian corn, or maize." Moses is not speaking here of gathering the corn (wheat) from the field, or the grapes from the vineyard. He is speaking about gathering up the corn from the threshing floor where it had been trampled to separate the grain from the hulls. The threshing of the wheat has been completed, the grapes have been pressed, and the grain is to be gathered off the threshing floor, the wine from the vat. Instead of saying it in these words, Moses used an idiomatic expression and said, "after thou hast gathered in thy goren (threshing floor) and thy yeqeb (winepress)."

The translators knew that yeqeb here referred to the winepress, but they also knew that the word wine also meant the freshly expressed juice that was in the winepress, and they used wine simply for smoothness of expression. In so doing they gave us more proof that the word wine means the freshly expressed juice, the must, in one of its several meanings.

Chapter 13

GATH — WINEPRESS

While there is no controversy over the word gath, I give the following that the reader may have a better picture of an ancient winepress. In my comments on yeqeb, I showed that a winepress consisted of two vats, an upper vat in which the grapes were pressed called the gath and a lower one which caught the juice flowing from the press and was called the yeqeb.

James Hamilton, in Fairbairn's imperial Standard Bible Encyclopedia, tells about Dr. Edward Robinson finding an ancient winepress, scooped out of the rock, on the road from Akka to Jerusalem. "Advantage had been taken of a ledge of rock; on the upper side, towards the south, a shallow vat had been dug out, eight feet square and fifteen inches deep, its bottom declining slightly towards the north. The thickness of rock left on the north was one foot; and two feet lower down on that side, another smaller vat was excavated, four feet square by three feet deep. The grapes were trodden in the shallow upper vat, and the juice drawn off by a hole at the bottom, still remaining, into the lower vat. This ancient press would seem to prove that in other days these hills were covered with vineyards; and such is its state of preservation that, were there still grapes in the vicinity, it might at once be brought into use without repair . . ."

This may be taken as a type of the Hebrew winepress. Like the Egyptians, the Jews may have employed wooden presses also; but these hewn out of the rock would be landmarks as permanent as threshing floors similarly constructed. Our modern methods of pressing the juice from the grapes are not much improved over the ancient method, and the human foot for pressing the juices from the grape without crushing the seeds still remains without a better substitute.

The winepresses were also used for pressing the oil from the olives. Joel 2:24, "And the floors shall be full of wheat, and the fats shall overflow with wine and oil."

This verse, though short in construction contains much meaning regarding the subject of unfermented wine. The time is prophesied when the harvest will be so plenteous that the fats (yeqeb, lower vat) will not be able to contain the juice (yayin) running from the press (gath, upper vat). The Hebrew word for wine here is yayin. Its use in this verse further establishes our position that the freshly expressed juice of the grape is yayin (sweet, unfermented wine). The one wine theory, that yayin always means fermented wine is refuted by this verse. The overflow was caused by the abundance of the juice (yayin) flowing from the press, fermentation having nothing to do in causing the overflow. It was the abundance that caused the overflow. The context shows this to be so.

49

Joel 3:15 also speaks of overflowing fats, "Put ye in the sickle, for the harvest is ripe: come, get you down; for the press (gath) is full, the fats (yeqeb) overflow; for their wickedness is great." We understand from this verse also that the yeqeb is the lower vat, and the gath is the upper one.

Chapter 14

MIMSAK — MIXED WINE

Mimsak (also spelled mimsach, mimesak, mamcak) appears twice in the Hebrew text and is rendered mixed wine once and drink offering the other time. Prov. 23:30, "They that go to seek mixed wine (mimsak)." Isa. 65:11, "But ye are they that forsake the Lord, that forget my holy mountain, that prepare a table for that troop (margin, or Gad), and that furnish the drink offering (mimsak) unto that number (margin, or Meni)."

Strong defines the word, "mixture, i.e. (spec.) wine mixed (with water or spices)." Young renders the word in Isa. 65:11 as drink offering, and in Prov. 23:30 defines it as anything mixed. According to Strong and Young it could be mixed with either water or spices.

The American Standard Version renders Isa. 65:11, "that fill mingled wine unto Destiny."

Douglas shows a relationship of mimsak with mesech and mezeg. "He says, Mesech, literally 'a mixture,' might be used in many senses; as in Pr. ix.2, the cognate verb occurs: Wisdom 'hath mingled her wine' — probably with water, according to a prevalent custom, though it might be with aromatics. But the noun appears to have been restricted in usage to a bad sense, to denote wine mingled with stupefying or exciting drugs, so that the wine might produce more powerful effects than was possible otherwise, at a time when distillation had not been yet discovered. The word mesech itself occurs only in Ps. lxxv.9 (8, English Version), 'it is full of mixture,' but a closely related form (mimsak), 'mixed wine,' Pr. 23.30, is undoubtedly the same, or so little different as to be now undistinguishable. And this latter word occurs again in Is. lxv.11, where it is rendered 'drink offering;' though this is not a translation, but a statement rightly enough inferred from the context. In the New Textament Greek a name occurs in a passage very similar to Ps. lxxv. 8, 'he shall drink of the wine of the wrath of God, which is poured out without mixture into the cup of his indignation,' Rev. xiv. 10; where again 'poured out' is rather an inference than a translation tou tekerasmenou akratou being literally 'which is mingled unmingled' with deleterious drugs in it, and undiluted. Still another kindred Hebrew word is Ca. vii. 3 (2 English Version), 'a round goblet which wanteth not liquor,' (mezeg) — understood by some to be wine mixed with water, by other to be aromatic wine; compare Ca. viii. 2, (yayin hareqahh), 'spiced wine.'"

The mixed wine of Bible times was not made by mixing different kinds of wines, but by mixing water or milk with the wine, which in many instances was the syrup or jam made by boiling the must, in order to make it thin enough for drinking; or by mixing spices or aromatics with the wine. These spices were used in different ways. At times they would add spices or aromatics to the must as it was being boiled to give flavor to the thick syrup or jam. At other times they would use spices or drugs to give fermented wine a more sedative effect. They did not have distilled drinks and the alcohol in fermented wine did not go higher than fourteen or fifteen percent. To make fermented wine more sedative or intoxicating these drugs were added and this was condemned by the writers of the Old Testament.

Chapter 15

SHEMARIM — DREGS OR PRESERVES?

Shemarim (also shehmakreem) is another Hebrew word that seems to be of uncertain meaning to the translators. It is used in such a way that, whatever its exact meaning may be, it will not affect the position of the Moderationists or of the Abstainers either way, but inasmuch as it is rendered wines in two instances, it is given place in this study to further illustrate the difficulty translators had in finding the proper rendering of Hebrew words related to our subject.

Zeph. 1:12, "And it shall come to pass at that time, that I will search Jerusalem with candles, and punish the men that are settled on their lees (shemarim): that say in their heart, The Lord will not do good, neither will he do evil." The margin shows that the Hebrew word rendered settled in this text also means curded or thickened.

Jer. 48:11, "Moab hath been at ease from his youth, and he hath settled on his lees (shemarim), and hath not been emptied from vessel to vessel, neither hath he gone into captivity: therefore his taste remained in him, and his scent is not changed."

Isa. 25:6, "And in this mountain shall the Lord of hosts make unto all people a feast of fat things, a feast of wines on the lees (shemarim), of fat things full of marrow, of wines on the lees (shemarim) well refined." Twice in this verse shemarim is rendered wines on the lees.

Ps. 75:8, "For in the hand of the Lord there is a cup, and the wine (chemer) is red; it is full of mixture; and he poureth out of the same: but the dregs (shemarim) thereof, all the wicked of the earth shall wring them out, and drink them." Two articles of drink are mentioned here. The chemer (red wine) is poured out; the dregs (shemarim) are left for the wicked to drink. From their use in this verse, it is evident that there is a difference in the meaning of these two words. The best, that which was on top, the chemer, was poured out, leaving the shemarim, the dregs on the bottom.

However, the use of shemarim in Isa. 25:6 would indicate that it has a second meaning similar to the meaning of chemer in Ps. 75:8. But when the two words are used together to convey a contrast they would not have similar meanings, but rather meanings of distinction or unlikeness.

The word lees comes from the French lie, meaning dregs, and from the Low Latin lia, a word of doubtful origin. It is a plural word and is used to indicate the grosser parts of the expressed juice which settles at the bottom of the vat. The finer juice is drawn off from the top for bottling.

In each of the above scriptures, shemarim is used in metaphorical senses: as a figure of how God is going to deal with the wicked; to describe the

53

indolent and slothful in Jerusalem and in Moab; and also to indicate how He is going to bless others. The indolent and slothful are pictured as that which has settled in the vat, the dregs; and that which the Lord is going to make the unrighteous drink is the dregs. The righteous are to have the best, the finer "wines on the lees well refined," which would be that which is on the top. The same word shemarim is used in each sentence. If it means dregs or settlings in the bottom of the vat in both usages, there would be no difference in the way God will deal with the wicked or the righteous.

Hitt says, "shem-mak-reem means preserves or jellies; some of the ancients preserved fruits being so thick they had to be scraped out of the containers and thinned with water before use."

Strong, who gives the spelling in the singular only, shemer not shemarim, says, "shemer," means "something preserved, i.e. the settlings (plur. only) of wine."

Young's Concordance, dealing with the word as it is rendered dregs, defines shemarim as preserves, dregs, lees. Where the word is rendered lees only, he defines shemarim merely as preserves. But in his dealing with wine where wines on the lees is given, he defines shemarim as "what is preserved sediment."

For Isa. 25:6, Moffatt reads, "Then on this hill of Sion for all nations the Lord of hosts will spread a banquet of rich food and of rare wines, of marrow dainties and of choice old wines." The New Catholic Bible renders it, "And the Lord of hosts shall make unto all people in this mountain a feast of fat things, a feast of wine, of fat things full of marrow, of wine purified from the lees.

Ferrar Fenton says, "Then the Great Lord will make for all tribes on this hill, A feast rich with marrow and well-prepared dainties, and grape juice well thickened by age."

Young's Literal Translation uses neither the word wine nor juice. "And made hath Jehovah of Hosts, For all the people on this mount, A banquet of fat things: Fat things full of marrow, preserved things refined." This is consistent with the definition of shemarim as preserves, which both he and Strong give.

Burns writes, "The passage in Isaiah xxv. 6, has been adverted to above. The ancient versions give very conflicting renderings of the Hebrew mista shemarim, 'a feast of preserves:' and the commentators are equally disagreed. The English translators have supplied the words 'wine on the' to give, as they imagined, a suitable rendering. Even retaining their conception of the sense, there is nothing to support the notion that the wine is eulogized because of an intoxicating quality. Wine, well-refined from its albuminous particles, and so preserved from fermentation, would admirably fulfill the conditions of the text."

The English rendering from the Septuagint Greek reads, "And the Lord of hosts shall make a feast for all the nations: on this mount they shall drink gladness, they shall drink wine." The Greek word for wine is oinon in this verse, and I have already shown that this is a generic word and grape syrup or jam here would very well come under the definition of something preserved.

From the renderings of shemarim in the King James Version it appears to be a word difficult to translate, but whatever its specific or generic meanings may be, its use in the Bible does not give the proponents of the use of fermented wine any help.

Samson differs with Strong and Young and says that shemarim indicates the juice in the wine-vat before it is drawn off to be stored. This does not deal with the sense of it being preserved, neither does it help to explain the reason for the contrasting use of the word in describing how God is going to reward the righteous and punish the wicked.

If the Hebrew text had read "yayin on the lees (shemarim)," or "tirosh on the lees," there would be no question about the meaning of Isa. 25:6, but the Hebrew uses the word shemarim only which the translators have rendered "wine on the lees," thus causing the difficulty or confusion.

We must keep in mind what has been stated before in this study that many times the meaning of words can be determined by the way the word is used in the sentence itself. This is especially so of words that have multiple meanings, and we must not ignore this in dealing with ancient languages. This is a principal respected in courts of jurisprudence, and we can get into difficulty if we fail to observe this rule.

Furthermore, words with limited and specific meanings are used many times in the Bible in a symbolic or metaphoric sense. "And he shall be like a tree planted by the rivers of water, that bringeth forth his fruit in his season; his leaf also shall not wither, and whatsoever he doeth shall prosper. The ungodly are not so: but are like the chaff which the wind driveth away" (Ps. 1:3,4). Does this mean the righteous are going to be turned into trees, have apples hanging from their branches, and bear leaves that last the year round? Does this mean the wicked are going to be turned into hulls that are left after the wheat has been threshed and be scattered over the field by the wind? Certainly not. These are words with specific meanings but are used in a symbolic sense. The meaning of the sentence must be determined, not by the dictionary definition of the word only, but also by the manner in which the word is used in the sentence. Similarly, the meaning of the words rendered wine in the Bible must be determined in many instances by their usage in the sentence. This is so of our study of Hebrew words in the Old Testament, and will be seen in our study of New Testament words.

Chapter 16

CHEMER — THE PURE BLOOD OF THE GRAPE

Chemer (also chemar, khemer, hhemer) is found two times in the Old Testament. It is the Hebrew equivalent for the Chaldee chamar, which also appears in the books of Ezra and Daniel.

This word is overlooked by many writers on wine. Hitt defines it as meaning "to boil up, froth, foam; referring to the action of the fresh fruit juice rushing out of the wine press." Young says it is "a thick sticky syrup." Burns says, "Khemer, in the passage named (Deut. xxxii. 14; Is. xxvii. 2), has obvious reference to natural unfermented wine."

The use of the word helps to clarify its meaning. Deut. 32 contains the song of Moses, in which he tells how God had dealt with Israel. Verses 13 and 14 read, "He made him ride on the high places of the earth, that he might eat the increase of the fields; and he made him to suck honey out of the rock, and oil out of the flinty rock; Butter of kine, and milk of sheep, with fat of lambs, and rams of the breed of Bashan, and goats, with the kidneys of wheat; and thou didst drink the pure (chemer) blood of the grape." Isa. 27:2, "In that day sing ye unto her, A vineyard of red wine (chemer)."

It is obvious that chemer in Isa. 27:2 could not refer to fermented wine. It is only after the juice has been pressed from the grapes and has had time to ferment, a process of many days, that it becomes fermented and intoxicating, but it is used here to indicate that which is still in the grape cluster in the vineyard. This could only refer to the grape itself or the sweet, fresh juice of the grape. That the word refers to the fresh grape juice is further seen by its use in Deut. 32:14, "the pure (chemer) blood of the grape." Fermented wine is not the pure blood of the grape. It is the corrupted juice of the grape, and the word "fermented" is associated with corruption in the Scriptures as we shall see later.

Other translations help us here on the meaning of chemer in this verse. The New Catholic Bible says, "the purest blood of the grape." Leeser, "and of the blood of the grape thou drankest unmixed wine." Rubin, "and of the blood of the grape thou drankest unmixed wine. Revised Standard Version, "and of the blood of the grape you drank wine." English Revised Version, "and of the blood of the grape thou drankest wine." Fenton, "Drank the foaming blood of the grape." Young, "And of the blood of the grape thou dost drink wine." Brenton's English translation of the Greek Septuagint, "and he drank wine, the blood of the grape." Fausset, "the blood of the grape, even wine."

These translations confirm the position of this writer and a host of other temperance writers that one meaning of the word wine is the juice or blood of the grape. The one wine theory, that if it is not fermented it is not wine, is completely refuted by these renderings of this one verse alone. The blood of the grape is that which runs out when the grape bursts its skin from ripeness, or when the grape is crushed in the vat. Fermented wine is not the blood of the grape. It especially is not the pure blood of the grape. Fermented wine is grape juice that has spoiled, has become corrupted by the turning of the sugar, which in some grapes may be as much as thirty percent, into alcohol, which may be as much as fourteen percent. There is no alcohol in the pure blood of the grape, but it does have a sugar content that varies in different grapes from fourteen to thirty percent. There is practically no sugar in wine that has gone through the complete fermenting process, seldom more than one-and-a-half to two percent. There are other substances in the pure blood of the grape that are not in fermented wine, and there are substances in the fermented wine that are not in the pure blood of the grape.

The expression pure blood of the grape, as it is rendered in the King James and other English versions, cannot refer to fermented wine, but it is wine —the sweet unfermented wine.

The New Catholic Bible says, "the purest blood of the grape." Nowhere in the Bible is fermentation associated with purity.

Chemer is the blood of the grape. The translators recognized it as wine. They rendered it so for two reasons. Chemer is the fresh, unfermented juice of the grape, and the fresh, unfermented juice of the grape is wine.

By design, the Lord Himself had these terms used together, chemer and the blood of the grape, so that we living in the twentieth century, when there is so much confusion on the subject, might come to a clear understanding of the truth.

Chapter 17

CHAMAR — CHALDEAN WINE

Chamar (also chemar, chamra, hhamar) is a Chaldean word found in Ezra and Daniel. It is akin to the Hebrew chemer which we have just considered, but we need to study both words. While chemer is found only twice in the Scriptures, and in both places refers to the unfermented grape juice, chamar is used more often and appears more generic in its meaning.

Young gives the same definition for chamar that he gives for chemer, stating that both words mean a thick sticky (mixed) syrup. Hitt defines it as the fresh pure fruit juice. It is obvious that the word has given commentators and translators difficulty for Samson says that it means intoxicating wines, but he fails to see or state that it is also used in a nonintoxicating sense.

Douglas treats both words together saying, "Hhamar occurs only in the Chaldee portions of the Old Testament, Ezr. vi.9; vii.22 and repeatedly in Da. v. But it is in accordance with the usual variation of Chaldee and Hebrew pronunciation to identify it with 'hhemer,' De. xxxii,14; Is. xxvii,2. In the latter text our translators have rendered it 'red wine,' referring no doubt to Ps. lxxv.9 (English Version), where the cognate verb occurs 'the wine is red,' although the preferable translation is 'the wine foams,' or perhaps, 'the wine is turbid,' for which respectable authority can be pleaded. In Deuteronomy the translation is, 'Thou didst drink the pure blood of the grape,' as if the word had been understood to mean the newly expressed grape-juice, of which we shall speak presently: and this is one of the senses in which we have noticed that yayin is taken. On the whole, we think it safest to regard hhamar as in Chaldee equivalent to yayin in Hebrew, the generic word for liquor obtained from grapes; and the rare word hhemer would be the corresponding form appearing only twice in Hebrew poetry, as is not unfrequent with words which are in common use in Chaldee prose."

According to Fausset, chamar is a generic word with one of its meanings being the pure blood of the grape, or the newly expressed grape juice. He further says, "Chamar is the Chaldee equivalent to Heb. Yayin, the generic term for grape liquor. It lit. means to foam (Deut. xxxii. 14, 'the blood of the grape, even wine,' not 'pure'): Ezra vi. 9, vii. 22; Can. v. 1; Isa. xxvii. 2."

The foaming action mentioned by Fausset, according to Hitt in his definition of chemer is "referring to the action of the fresh fruit juice rushing out of the wine press." Some have erroneously taken the foaming action to mean fermentation.

The use of the word in Ezra and Daniel indicates that chamar may be either fermented or unfermented. The wine that Daniel, Shadrach, Meshach and Abednego refused to drink in Dan. 1:5, 8, 16 is given the Hebrew name yayin. But the wine in Belshazzar's fateful banquet in Daniel 5 was called by the Chaldee word chamar. Dan. 5:1, 2, "Belshazzar the king made a great feast to a thousand of his lords, and drank wine (chamar) before the thousand. Belshazzar, whiles he tasted the wine (chamar), commanded to bring the golden and silver vessels which his father Nebuchadnezzar had taken out of the temple which was in Jerusalem; that the king, and his princes, his wives, and his concubines, might drink therein."

These vessels had not been used for drinking intoxicants and Belshazzar's action here was one of defiance of the God of Israel for verse 4 says, "They drank wine (chamar), and praised the gods of gold, and of silver, of brass, of iron, of wood, and of stone." This is given by Daniel as the reason for God's anger against Belshazzar. Verse 23, "But thou hast lifted up thyself against the lord of heaven; and they have brought the vessels of his house before thee, and thou, and thy lords, thy wives, and thy concubines, have drunk wine (chamar) in them; and thou hast praised the gods of silver, and gold, of brass, iron, wood, and stone, and which see not, nor hear, nor know: and the God in whose hand thy breath is, and whose are all thy ways, hast thou not known."

In these verses, chamar has a use inconsistent with sobriety and true worship. Certainly those who advocate the use of fermented wine can take no comfort from these scriptures which associate it with blasphemy and idolatry. To avoid such things the four Hebrews refused to take the king's wine and the fermented wine advocates would do well to follow their example.

Chamar is used again in Ezra where Darius orders that provisions be given to the elders of the Jews so they can return to Jerusalem to rebuild the house of God and offer sacrifices.

Ezra 6:9, "And that which they have need of, both young bullocks, and rams, and lambs, for the burnt offerings of the God of heaven, wheat, salt, wine (chamar), oil, according to the appointment of the priests which are at Jerusalem, let it be given them day by day without fail: That they may offer sacrifices of sweet savours unto the God of heaven, and pray for the life of the king and of his sons."

Chamar is used finally in Ezra 7:21-23, "And I Artaxerxes the king, do make a decree to all the treasures which are beyond the river, that whatsoever Ezra the priest, the scribe of the law of the God of heaven, shall require of you, it be done speedily. Unto an hundred talents of silver, and to an hundred measures of wheat, and to an hundred baths of wine (chamar), and to an hundred baths of oil, and salt without prescribing measure. Whatsoever is commanded by the God of heaven, let it be diligently done for the house of the God of heaven: for why should there be wrath against the realm of the king and his sons?"

A number of points should be kept in mind when studying the use of the word chamar. First of all, it is a generic word, and while its use in Daniel indicates that it may mean fermented wine at times, that is not its sole meaning. We have already seen that it means the fresh juice of the grape.

Secondly, this wine was to be used by the priests as they ministered in offering sacrifices, and they were forbidden to drink wine or strong drink when so ministering. Lev. 10:8-11, "And the Lord spake unto Aaron, saying, Do not drink wine nor strong drink, thou, nor thy sons with thee, when ye go into the tabernacle of the congregation, lest ye die: it shall be a statute for ever throughout your generations: and that ye may put difference between holy and unholy, and between unclean and clean; And that ye may teach the children of Israel all the statutes which the Lord hath spoken unto them by the hand of Moses."

It would not be consistent for Darius or Artaxerxes to furnish the priests with articles to use in offering sacrifices when God Himself had forbidden the priests to partake of these same articles when so ministering.

The reason for the prohibition is clearly stated in Lev. 10:8-11, "...that ye may put difference between holy and unholy, and between unclean and clean; And that ye may teach the children of Israel all the statutes which the Lord hath spoken unto them by the hand of Moses." This is similar to the decree in Prov. 31:4, 5, "It is not for kings, O Lemuel, it is not for kings to drink wine; nor for princes strong drink; Lest they drink, and forget the law, and pervert the judgement of any of the afflicted."

Of course, it would be that which was fermented that would cause kings to forget the law, princes to pervert the judgement of the afflicted, and render priests unable to put difference between holy and unholy, and between unclean and clean. Would God, who forbad priests, kings and princes to drink that which would render him unable to properly execute the law and distinguish between the holy and unholy, accept the same as an offering of "sacrifice of sweet savours unto the God of heaven."

All of the ceremony, ritual, religious ordinances, sacrifices, shedding of blood, washings, fastings, circumcision of the Old Testament served in one way or another to signify, symbolize, foreshadow, or be a substitute for some aspect of the redemptive work of the coming Christ.

This is particularly so of the blood offerings, and the sprinkling of the blood of the Passover Lamb. On the night of the Last Supper, when the Lord and His disciples observed the Passover, He took the cup and said, "This is my blood of the new testament, which is shed for the remission of sins" (Matt. 26:28; Mark 14:24; Luke 22:19, 20; 1 Cor. 11:25,26).

Seven hundred years before Christ, Isaiah prophesied of His death and resurrection as "an offering for sin" (Isa. 53); and three hundred years before Isaiah's time, David prophesied of Christ's resurrection, "For thou wilt not leave my soul in hell; neither wilt thou suffer thine Holy One to see corruption" (Ps. 16:10). On the Day of Pentecost, Peter quoted this verse in Acts 2:27, "Because thou wilt not leave my soul in hell, neither wilt thou suffer thine Holy One to see corruption," applying it to the Lord's death and resurrection. Neither the flesh nor the blood of Christ saw corruption.

The Apostle wrote in 1 Pet. 1:18,19, "For as ye know ye were not redeemed with corruptible things, as silver and gold, from your vain conversation (behaviour, manner of life) received by tradition from your fathers; But with the precious blood of Christ, as of a lamb without blemish and without spot."

61

We are redeemed by the incorruptible blood of Jesus Christ, and anything that is used to typify, symbolize, signify His blood must also be without corruption. The Passover bread, to properly symbolize His flesh, had to be unfermented. Similarly, for wine to symbolize the blood of Christ, it must be the uncorrupted, unfermented, pure blood of the grape. It will be shown later that the word unleavened should be unfermented.

Now, getting back to the subject of our present consideration, it is inconceivable to this writer that God, who was so particular in requiring that everything that had any ferment, which is corruption, be removed from the house during the Passover season would permit the offering of corrupted or fermented wine on His altar of sacrifice. Ezra 6:14 states that all that was done in the return to Jerusalem and the restoration of the temple and the offering of sacrifices was "according to the commandment of the God of Israel."

The One Wine Theorists must face the question, "Would God forbid the use of anything fermented during the Passover Supper, which served to typify Jesus our Passover Lamb, and then accept what was forbidden at Passover as a "sacrifice of sweet savours" (verse 9) at another time?

To say that God would command an intoxicating, corrupted, fermented wine to symbolize the shedding of the blood of His son in preference to the sweet, unfermented, uncorrupted blood of the grape, when His Word contains so many maledictions against fermented wine, and His priests, kings and princes were forbidden to use it, is unthinkable.

But if an hundred baths of chamar in the form of unfermented grape juice were given for a sacrifice of sweet savours to God there would be no conflict with any of His commandments.

This writer cannot accept the thought of sacrificial wine being fermented.

Chapter 18

OINOS AND NEW TESTAMENT WINE

Oinos is the Greek equivalent of the Hebrew yayin (also yain), and its meaning is just as generic as the Hebrew word.

Young's definition of oinos is simply "grape juice." Strong defines it as, "a primitive word (of perhaps Hebrew origin yayin); 'wine' (literally or figuratively." Thayer's Greek Lexicon says, "oinos, -ou, o, [from Homer down], Septuagint for yayin, also for tirosh (mush, new wine), chemer, etc. wine."

I have shown that yayin is a generic word meaning the grape itself, grape raisins, the grape juice unfermented, grape syrup, grape jam, and grape juice fermented. I have shown that tirosh means the grape itself, or the unfermented grape juice, but never fermented. I have shown that chemer is the blood of the grape. By the use of oinos in the Septuagint as the Greek equivalent of these words, it is clear that oinos means all that these Hebrew words mean.

Douglas does not list the word oinos except in his definition of yayin, in which definition he shows the meaning of both the Hebrew and Greek words. In the chapter on yayin I gave his definition, but I repeat it here for the convenience of the reader. Douglas says, "Certainly the word is found to be very widespread, as in the Greek oinos, the Latin vinum, &c. This Hebrew word is said to occur 141 times in the Old Testament, and the Greek word 32 times in the New, besides words derived from it. It seems to be used to describe 'all sorts of wine,' N. v. 18, from the simple grape juice, or a thickened syrup, to the strongest liquors with which the Israelites were acquainted, the use of which often led to deplorable scenes of drunkenness." Notice that Douglas gives "the simple grape juice, or thickened syrup" as two of the meanings of both words.

Samson shows that oinos is used to translate tirosh which is never fermented or intoxicating, and therefore oinos too is not intoxicating in many of its usages, and further says that oinos covers every variety of wine as is demonstrated, "First, from usage in classic Greek; second, from the Greek translation used by Christ and his apostles, in which tirosh, which had no intoxicating element is generally rendered oinos; third, from the Latin terms used in allusion to unfermented wines described by roman writers from Cato (B.C. 200) to Pliny (A.D. 100); fourth, from the usage of Mark, who, writing for Romans familiar with their own unfermented wines, calls the beverage offered to Christ when nailed to the cross oinos (15:23), while Matthew uses the term oxos, still called in French vin-gar, sour wine; though in vingar, the last natural and divinely-ordered product of grape-juice, the alcohol developed in the temporary process of fermentation is converted into acetic acid."

It may be helpful to consider the word vinegar here. Samson seems to be using an older French variant of the word. The New American Encyclopedic Dictionary, Vol. 5, gives this definition of the English word, "vinegar, vineger, vinegre, vynegre, s. & a. [Lit=sour wine, from Fr. vinaigre=vinegar, from vin=wine, and aigre=sharp, sour.]" Our English word vinegar is derived from the French vinaigre, and in both languages the word means sour wine. Vinegar is wine that has passed through the complete process of spoiling.

First it was wine unfermented. Then it became wine fermented. Finally it became wine soured. But in each stage it was wine. In the second stage, the sugar in the fresh juice had turned to carbon dioxide and alcohol. In the third stage, the alcohol had turned into acetic acid. At first it was sweet, then fermented, and then sour, but wine always. Vinegar is sour wine.

The One Wine Theorists face the problem of harmonizing this with their position that wine is always and only fermented grape juice.

In defining Hebrew and Greek words and their variants in other languages I use the word cognate quite often. This word is defined as: allied by blood, of or proceding from the same stock or root, of the same or similar nature, related or cognate languages.

With this understanding of the word cognate, we can appreciate the employment of the word by Samson in the following statement, "As all lexicographers allow, yayin is cognate with Greek oinos, Latin vinum, Italian and Spanish vino, French vin, German wein, and English 'wine'." The full import of this statement is very significant. What yayin (yain) means in Hebrew; oinos means in Greek, vinum means in Latin, vino means in Italian and Spanish, vin means in French, wein means in German, and wine means in English.

Ernest Gordon, commenting on oinos as a proper rendering of the Hebrew tirosh (unfermented wine), says, "In the Septuagint the Hebrew word for grape juice, tirosh, is translated at least 33 times by the Greek word oinos, wine, and the adjective 'new' is not present. Oinos without qualification then can in the New Testament easily mean unfermented wine."

In the chapter on yayin, Fenton's definition of both yayin and oinos is given and will not be repeated here except to say that he has defined both as generic words which mean: the grapes, raisins, non-intoxicating syrup, conserve, jam, unfermented juice, fermented grape juice, and was also used to denote various kinds of drinks or confections of other fruits in addition to the grape.

Hitt says, "Greek — Oynos, a generic term, and Hebrew Yah-yin include sweet wine, unmixed pure grape juice, glucose, or very pure wine and the like; neos, or new, distinguished it from the old or fermented wine."

The fact that the Seventy Greek and Hebrew scholars who translated the Hebrew Scriptures into the Greek, 280 B.C., in what is known as the Septuagint Version of the Old Testament, employed the word oinos in translating tirosh, which has been shown as never meaning fermented wine, is proof that two of the meanings of oinos is the unfermented juice of the grape, and the grape itself.

The one wine theory, that the Hebrew yayin, the Greek oinos, and the English wine, invariably mean just one kind of wine, the fermented grape juice, and that these words are not generic terms with multiple meanings receives its death blow from Neh. 5:18, "Now that which was prepared for me daily was one ox and six choice sheep; also fowls were prepared for me, and once in ten days store of all sorts of wine." The Hebrew word here is yayin. "All sorts of yayin." In the Septuagint Greek Version the word is oinos, and the English translation reads, "and every ten days wine (oinos) in abundance of all sorts." Not just one sort of wine (yayin, oinos). All sorts, this is an all-inclusive expression. I have shown that the words yayin and oinos are generic terms having multiple meanings, and with the words all sorts added this verse sounds the death toll to the one wine theory.

No greater mistake was ever made in Biblical interpretation than the unwarranted assumption, in the face of such evidence to the contrary, that the words yayin, oinos, and wine as used in the Old and New Testaments and in the Septuagint, always mean a fermented, intoxicating beverage.

It is essential that this misunderstanding be corrected for unless we understand that these are generic words and unfermented grape juice is one of their multiple meanings we shall never grasp the true meaning of dozens of Bible texts.

"All sorts of wine (yayin, oinos)" would include grapes, raisins, syrup, jam, and unfermented grape juice.

Chapter 19

SIKERA — CIDER, PALM SAP AND SUGAR

Sikera, the Greek word which is cognate with the Hebrew shekar appears only once in the New Testament. Luke 1:15, "For he shall be great in the sight of the Lord and shall drink neither wine nor strong drink" (sikera).

Wycliff's Translation reads, "He schal not drinke wyn and sydir."

I have already shown that modern dictionaries list sikera as the Greek equivalent of our English sugar, and that the New American Encyclopedic Dictionary gives it as the Greek word for cider.

I have further shown that sikera is the Greek equivalent of the Hebrew shekar, having all the several meanings that belong to the Hebrew word including sugar, cider, palm sap unfermented, palm sap fermented, etc.

Of the 22 times the Hebrew word shekar appears in the Old Testament, the Septuagint Greek Version of the Old Testament uses the word sikera 12 times.

Young's definition sustains our position that the word may denote a beverage that is either fermented or unfermented. Under "strong drink," Young first shows that the Hebrew word shekar means, "Sweet drink (what satiates or intoxicates), shekar." Here he shows that shekar does not always mean a fermented or intoxicating drink. It is a drink that satiates, which means to fully satisfy. Both words derive from the same Latin word, satisfacere, satis meaning enough and facere meaning to do or to make. To satiate means to supply fully. After saying "what satiates," Young adds "or intoxicates." He then gives the Old Testament references. Next he gives the Greek word sikera and shows that it may or that it may not be fermented, "Sweet drink, (often fermented), sikera, shekar Hebrew."

According to Young, both shekar and sikera mean first of all a sweet drink. This very well applies to both palm sap and sweet cider. Often fermented also applies to both palm sap and cider. But often fermented does not mean always fermented. Often means frequently occurring, and that suggests what is exceptional rather than the general rule.

Sikera is the Greek equivalent for the Hebrew shekar and has all the several meanings of shekar.

Chapter 20

GLEUKOS — NEW WINE, MUST, FRESH GRAPE JUICE

Gleukos appears only once in the New Testament. Acts 2:13, "Others mocking said, These men are full of new wine (gleukos)."

Thayer's Greek Lexicon defines this word as, "Must, the sweet juice pressed from the grape." Young says, "Sweet or new wine." Hitt says the word means, "Latin mustum, English must; meaning sweet or new grape juice." Douglas writes, "For gleukos is unquestionably must." McClintock and Strong show the meaning of gleukos in their definition of tirosh as, "... 'sweet wine,' (in Mic. vi. 15), properly signifies must, the freshly pressed juice of the grape (the gleukos or sweet wine of the Greeks, rendered 'new wine' in Acts ii. 13)."

Gleukos is the newly expressed, unfermented juice of the grape. The word used by Wycliff in his translation of gleukos in Acts 2:13 is must. "Others scorned and saiden for these men ben ful of must." The Latin Vulgate translates the word gleukos in this verse as musto. The Septuagint Greek Version uses the word glukasmon for the Hebrew asis, which means the fresh juice of the grape, in Joel 3:18, "the mountains shall drop new wine (Hebrew asis, Greek glukasmon)," and in Amos 9:13, "and the mountains shall drop sweet wine (Hebrew asis, Greek glukasmon)." It is apparent that the Seventy in the year 280 B.C. understood that the word gleukos was the Greek equivalent for the Hebrew asis which means the sweet, fresh juice of the grape.

Must is an Anglo Saxon word. The German cognate is most, and the Latin is mustum which means the expressed, unfermented juice of the grape as we shall see later according to the best modern dictionaries.

In addition to its application to the fresh grape juice, must also was applied to the freshly expressed juice of the apple or pear. So it also conveyed the meaning of cider. But must is always unfermented.

The Latins, understanding that the Greek word gleukos denoted what was unfermented, used mustum as its Latin equivalent.

Funk & Wagnalls Desk Standard Dictionary gives the meaning of the Greek gleukos as must, sweet wine, in its definition of our English word glukos, which is derived from the Greek.

It is beyond question that gleukos is never fermented, even as must is never fermented, both words denoting the fresh grape juice that flows into the lower vat during the pressing, or is preserved in its sweet and unfermented form.

Chapter 21

JOSEPH'S INTERPRETATION OF THE CUPBEARER'S DREAM ACCORDING TO FLAVIUS JOSEPHUS THE JEWISH HISTORIAN

Flavius Josephus was the famous Jewish historian who was born in the year 37 A.D., just four years after the crucifixion of Jesus. He lived and wrote his works during the times of the Apostles, and was well acquainted with the expression, idioms, practices of the Jews in Apostolic times, and had a thorough knowledge of the history of ancient Israel.

Josephus tells us that as far back as the times of the Pharaohs of ancient Egypt it was the practice to squeeze the juice out of the grapes into the cup and immediately drink it fresh as a part of the meal thus confirming what is stated in Genesis 40:11.

In his Antiquities of the Jews, Book II, Chap. V, Par. 2, Josephus writes about the dream of Pharaoh's cupbearer who had been imprisoned with Joseph, and the interpretation that Joseph gave of his dream, "He therefore said that in his sleep he saw three clusters of grapes hanging upon three branches of a vine, large already, and ripe for gathering; and that he squeezed them into a cup which the king held in his hand; and when he had strained the wine, he gave it to the king to drink, and that he received it from him with a pleasant countenance. This, he said, was what he saw; and he desired Joseph, that if he had any portion of understanding in such matters, he would tell him what his vision foretold. Who bid him be of good cheer, and expect to be loosed from his bonds in three day's time, because the king desired his service, and was about to restore him to it again; for he let him know that God bestows the fruit of the vine upon men for good; which wine is poured out to him, and is the pledge of fidelity and mutual confidence among men; and put an end to their quarrels, takes away passion and grief out of the minds of them that use it, and makes them cheerful. Thou sayest that thou didst squeeze this wine from three clusters of grapes with thine hands, and that the king received it: know, therefore, that this vision is for thy good, and foretells a relapse from thy present distress within the same number of days as the branches had whence thou gatheredst thy grapes in thy sleep."

Josephus wrote in the Greek language. In writing about the juice that was squeezed from the three clusters of grapes, he used the Greek word gleukos. Whiston, who translated Josephus into English used the word wine in translating the Greek gleukos. (See Whiston's Translation in Josephus, Page 65.)

There are a number of truths revealed in this incident. Nineteen hundred years before Christ, and 400 years before Israel became a nation at Mt.

Sinai, it was the custom to squeeze the juice from grapes and drink it immediately in its fresh, unfermented state. This was what Josephus called gleukos, which our English translators render wine in Acts 2:13. Does not this establish the fact of an unfermented wine? It is not fermented, but it is wine.

Whiston's translation of Josephus was published in 1737 A.D., at a time when English dictionaries were defining wine as the juice of the grape, and Whiston used the word wine to translate gleukos because in his day wine meant the fresh juice of the grape as well as the fermented. Unfermented juice is wine.

The juice of the grape was gleukos before it was squeezed out. It was gleukos after it was squeezed out. Wine was a proper rendering of the word gleukos in the time of Whiston, and also the time of the King James translators, and both he and the King James translators used wine for translating gleukos.

Josephus also called this the fruit of the vine, the same expression used by our Lord at the Last Supper. This establishes that the fruit of the vine is the sweet, unfermented juice of the grape, and that gleukos also is the sweet, unfermented juice of the grape, the fruit of the wine.

The Hebrews had several words which were used for the fruit of the vine, among which are asis, tirosh, yain. The Greeks called it oinos and gleukos. The Romans called it vinum and mustum.

Fuerst and Gesenius, the Hebrew-German Lexicographers, called it most and ungegorener Wein in German. In English we call it must and unfermented wine. The King James translators used the word wine without using the word unfermented because they knew that the word wine included that sense.

Josephus was living at the same time when Matthew, Mark, and Luke wrote their Gospels telling about Jesus, at the Last Supper, using the expression the fruit of the vine. If the fruit of the vine meant unfermented grape juice to Josephus, why should it mean anything else to Jesus, or the Apostles, or to us?

More authorities could be cited to show that gleukos means the fresh grape juice, or must, but we must stop somewhere.

When the mockers, on the Day of Pentecost, said the 120 were "full of new wine," they used the Greek word gleukos (Acts 2:13). Wycliff's Translation says, "Others scorned and saiden for these ben ful of must." The Latin Vulgate uses the Latin word musto.

This was said in mockery. It was a taunt. The mockers knew that gleukos was not intoxicating. Neither were they sincere in their taunt. Had they really believed the disciples were drunk, they would have used a word indicating fermented wine. The reason behind the use of gleukos is that the ridicule was made all the more taunting by the use of incongruous terms. People do not get intoxicated on sweet grape juice, so these incongruous terms were used for the purpose of exciting all the more laughter. The total abstinence of Jesus and His disciples was no doubt a known fact. The taunt was tantamount to accusing a present day temperance speaker of being intoxicated on lemonade. They were incompatible terms used for provoking more laughter than would have been provoked by merely accusing the disciples of being drunk on fermented wine.

It has been argued by fermented wine advocates that gleukos here could not possibly mean fresh, unfermented juice because Pentecost is separated from the grape harvest by eight months and the unfermented juice of the grape would not have kept that long without fermenting, and in those days they had no methods of preserving the juice in its unfermented state. Consequently, the 120 could not have been drinking unfermented grape juice. The statement, therefore, that they were full of gleukos can only mean they had been drinking intoxicating wine.

This argument overlooks the fact that the taunt was what the mockers said about the 120, and not what the facts really were. The facts were that they had neither been drinking unfermented wine nor fermented wine. They were not full of gleukos. "They were all filled with the Holy Ghost" (Acts 2:4). This argument is further overthrown by the fact that, contrary to the false notion that there were no known methods of preventing fermentation and preserving the juice in its sweet state, there were several well known and widely used methods of preservation which will be taken up later.

Chapter 22

MUST DEFINED

We have used the word must quite often in these pages when considering the meaning of Hebrew and Greek words. It will be helpful to give a bit of space here to the word itself, for the definition of must alone is a refutation of the one wine theory, that grape juice must be fermented before it is wine.

The Reader's Digest Encyclopedic Dictionary, which includes Funk & Wagnalls Standard College Dictionary, defines must as, "The pressed unfermented juice of the grape or other fruit. [OE'L mustum (vinum) new (wine)]."

The New American Encyclopedic Dictionary defining must says, "Anglo must, from Latin mustum=new wine, properly neuter singular of mustus = young, fresh, new." Then in its definition of the English word it goes on to say, "The unfermented juice of the grape; expressed for making wine." Notice that the Latin mustum, from which our English word derives, means new wine. It is wine before fermentation has had time to do its work.

Funk & Wagnalls Family Dictionary defines the word thus, "1 The expressed unfermented juice of the grape. 2 Unfermented potato pulp. Old English, Latin mustum, new wine."

Webster's Collegiate Dictionary, 3rd and 5th Editions both give the same definition, "[AS. must fr. L. mustum (sc. vinum), fr. mustus young fresh.] The expressed juice of the grape, or other fruit, before fermentation; new wine."

In all these definitions must is the unfermented juice of the grape and that grape juice is new wine. It is wine even though not fermented.

Webster's Collegiate Dictionary, 7th Edition gives this definition, "[ME, fr. OE, fr. L mustum]: the expressed juice of grapes or other fruit before and during fermentation." Grape juice is must before fermentation. It is must during fermentation. But it is not must after fermentation. So fermented wine is not must.

This is significant for the Latin Vulgate, which was translated from the Greek by Jerome in the years 383-405 A.D., used the word musto in translating the Greek gleukos in Acts 2:13, instead of the word vinum.

As I write this, we have a young lady visiting in our home from Freiburg, Germany, Miss Elfi Baer, a registered nurse. I asked Elfi what the German word would be for the fresh juice just pressed from the grape, and her reply was, "Most." I asked her what the meaning of ungegorener wein is and she said it means, "Unfermented wine." The reader will remember that the Hebrew-German Lexicographers, Fuerst and Gesenius used ungegorener wein to translate the Hebrew tirosh, they also used the word most.

75

I pointed out earlier in this study the tendency in modern dictionaries to alter the meaning of the word wine from its original meaning, and limiting it to mean the fermented grape juice only. Again we see this tendency in the 7th Edition of Webster's Collegiate Dictionary. No mention is made in this edition of must, the unfermented grape juice, being new wine as both the 3rd and 5th editions stated. It does not say that must is not new wine. It merely leaves out that part of the definition which was given in the previous editions.

From what is given above, it is clear that must is the fresh grape juice that is not fermented, and that juice is new wine. It is wine although it is not fermented. The word new was used to indicate that it was recently pressed from the grape. Now if that new wine were preserved in its original state, without fermentation, it would still be wine although it would not be new.

Chapter 23

WHY THE TRANSLATORS USED THE WORD WINE

To most English speaking people the word wine means the fermented, alcoholic, intoxicating juice of the grape or other fruit. Many Bible Commentators have fallen into this error. Even E. W. Bullinger, who produced the Companion Bible, a fine work with many helpful notes and comments, writes, ". . .with these data it will be seen that the modern expression, 'unfermented wine,' is a contradiction of terms. If it is wine, it must have fermented. If it has not been fermented, it is not wine, but a syrup."

This was not the understanding of the meaning of wine by the King James translators and other English translators who preceded them. I repeat what I have said elsewhere in this treatise, that what a word means today, and what it meant 350 years ago, and what it meant in ancient times may be different things. Many words commonly used when the King James Version was being prepared have a much different meaning in this last quarter of the twentieth century.

"For the mystery of iniquity doth already work: only he who now letteth will let, until he be taken out of the way" (2 Thes. 2:7). In the years 1604-1611, when the King James Version was being produced, the words letteth and let meant to hinder. Today we understand the word means to permit. A good dictionary will show that both definitions are correct, but the hindrance meaning is now archaic.

The meaning of the word prevent has similarly undergone a change. "We which are alive and remain unto the coming of the Lord shall not prevent them which are asleep" (1 Thes. 4:15). Four centuries ago this word meant to proceed, to go before. This meaning is now archaic and we understand the word to mean frustrate, forestall, keep from happening.

Similarly, the word wine has gone through a change of meaning in the last two hundred years.

We must also keep in mind that some words have a specific and a generic meaning. This is so with the Hebrew words yayin, tirosh, and the Greek oinos. Our English word wine is a translation of the Greek oinos and the Hebrew yayin, but it is more than a translation. A study of the etymology of the word shows that wine is derived from oinos and yayin, and in its early usage meant what the original words that it derives from meant. Just as yayin and oinos were generic terms with multiple meanings, even so our English word wine is a generic word with multiple meanings.

This is also true of the German word wein. Ungegorener wein means unfermented wine. Even though it is unfermented it is still wine.

Our English word has become perverted to have only one meaning to most people. If we adhere strictly to the present specific meaning of wine, we can only condemn our English translators and say they were wrong in many uses of the word. In my earlier writings, I had done this, but now I must confess that I was wrong and they were right, for, if we recognize that the word in its original usage was a generic term with several meanings, we can understand why they used it in places where we would not use it today, and their use of the word was proper according to the meanings of the word when they did their translating.

They had more knowledge of the true meaning of the word than we have today, and this accounts for the way they applied it in their translations. They are not to be condemned for our ignorance of the meanings of the word. Temperance writers would do well to recognize this rather than to condemn the translators in many instances.

In the year 1604, one archbishop, eight bishops, and eight deans of the Church of England, with four leaders of the Puritan party, and the learned Dr. John Reynolds of Oxford assembled with and at the invitation of King James. It was decided at this meeting that a new version of the Scriptures would be produced. Fifty-four men were appointed, although only forty-seven actually engaged in the work to revise The Bishop's Bible.

Fifteen rules were adopted to govern their labors. Rule One provided, "The ordinary Bible read in the Church, commonly called 'The Bishop's Bible' to be followed, and as little altered as the truth of the original will permit." This rule limited the translators to follow the pattern set by The Bishop's Bible. The Bishop's Bible was a revision of the Great Bible, which was based on The Thomas Matthew Bible, and it was a revision of Tyndale's Bible which first appeared in 1525. So by Rule One, Tyndale's Bible, Thomas Matthew's Bible, the Great Bible, and the Bishop's Bible all had an influence on the King James Version. But we must also mention that the Geneva Bible had a great influence on these translators. By Rule One, the pattern which the translators were to follow had already been set.

Rule Four provided, "When a word hath divers significations, that to be kept which hath been most commonly used by the ancient fathers, being agreeable to the propriety of the place and the analogy of the faith." This rule would certainly apply to the words yayin, oinos, and wine, all of which have divers significations. In many places where the words grape juice, must, unfermented wine, raisins would have made the meaning clearer to twentieth century readers, they translated the Hebrew yayin and the Greek oinos with the one English word that had the same divers significations and used the word wine. They did not do their work according to definitions of English words in the last quarter of the twentieth century, but according to the divers significations of words in their day.

Rule Six provided, "No marginal notes at all to be affixed, but only for the explanation of the Hebrew or Greek words which cannot, without some circulocution, so briefly and fitly be preserved in the text." Accordingly, it seems that the translators did not consider it necessary in their day to provide explanatory notes on yayin, tirosh, or oinos because they felt the word wine was sufficient.

Governed by these rules, and understanding the divers significations of yayin, oinos, and their own English word wine, the translators did only what they would be expected to do and employed the word wine. It was the only word they had which expressed in the English language the divers significations of the words they were translating.

At times they did use words that have caused confusion, such as strong drink for the word shekar. Although their English words cider and sugar derived from shekar, and palm sap would have been a proper rendering, they used the words strong drink instead, which has caused confusion in regard to Deut. 14:26 and other texts. They were in error at times, but not so much as would appear to those who do not understand the divers significations of the words they were dealing with.

The translators knew that wine may be unfermented or fermented. The divers significations of wine are established by the two German scholars, William Gesenius and William Fuerst (also Furst). Both of these men produced Hebrew-German Lexicons. In both of their lexicons the Hebrew word tirosh is rendered ungegorener wein, which in English means unfermented wine. They had no hesitancy in using the word ungegorener (unfermented) along with the word wein. It was wine even though not fermented. Apparently in German the word wein had divers significations as well as in English.

In the chapter on yayin, I showed that the English word wine (archaic win, wyn, wyne) derived from the Hebrew yayin (yain), which is a universal word: Greek oinos, Ethiopian wain, Armenian gini, Latin vinum, German wein, Welsh gwin, Gaelic fion, Anglo-Saxon win, Gothic wein, Old High German win, Icelandic vin, Dutch wign, Swedish vin, Danish viin, Old Irish fin, Italian vino, French vin, etc.

Again we quote the American Ecclesiastical Review, in 1898, "Yayin is wine generally, new or old, fermented or unfermented, but usually the latter. The Hebrew letter YOD (consonant) in the beginning of a word answers to a W in related languages, and the word for wine is actually the same in Hebrew, Greek, English and several other languages, with but a slight difference in pronunciation."

Ernest Gordon writes, "Dr. Lyman Abbott was in his day no friend of the anti-alcohol movement, yet he can be considered a reasonably competent scholar." It is from Abbott's Dictionary of Religious Knowledge that the following quotation is made, "Fermented wine was the least common (in Biblical times) and the percentage of alcohol was small. New wines were wholly without alcohol and were easily preserved in this condition for several months. There were also wines in which, by boiling or by drugs, the process of fermentation was prevented and alcohol excluded. These were mixed with water and constituted the most common drink of the land" (P. 973).

The ancient Hebrews had a well understood word that was all expressive and denoted the product of the vine in all of its different states including the grape itself, dried raisins, the freshly expressed unfermented juice, the juice boiled to prevent fermentation, the juice cooked down to a syrup, the juice cooked further into a jam, and the juice that had fermented and was alcoholic. That word was yayin.

The Greeks had a word just as expressive and which was cognate to the Hebrew word. The Greek word was oinos. The Romans had a word just as expressive, vinum. The Germans had a word, wein.

Coming down to the years 1604 to 1611, when the King James Version was being prepared, did the English language have a word? Yes. It was the same word that earlier English translators had used, and as the Greek, Latin, and German words all derived from the Hebrew yayin, so did the English word. That word was wine.

No doubt the English translators felt their word expressed more than any other word in the English language the meaning of the Hebrew yayin and the Greek oinos, and it did.

As the Israelites understood their word and used it accordingly, and as the Greeks understood their word and used it accordingly, and as the Romans understood their word and used it accordingly, so the King James translators understood their word and used it accordingly.

Unfortunately, in our day, these words are not understood by most writers and Bible expositors, and the average reader receives his information on our subject from men who are not properly informed. It is disappointing indeed to witness the superficial manner in which the wines of the Bible have been treated by men who have earned the right to be respected and acknowledged as authorities in other areas of Biblical interpretation, but on this subject their knowledge is so deficient.

When all the facts concerning the way the King James Version was produced are better known, we can understand more fully the reasons why the translators used the word wine as they did, and we shall also have more appreciation for their Version, and also for the men themselves.

Chapter 24

WAS THE SACRAMENTAL WINE OF THE BIBLE FERMENTED?

Did Jesus serve sweet grape juice or fermented wine to His disciples at the Last Supper? Should Christians use grape juice or fermented wine for Communion?

The Christian Church is divided on this subject. Some denominations use sweet grape juice. Other denominations use fermented wine. Still others make it a matter of choice for the local assembly.

Advocates of unfermented grape juice give several reasons for insisting that the cup Jesus served His disciples did not contain fermented wine, but held the sweet grape juice, and this is what should be used in the Communion Service today.

Those who advocate the use of fermented wine are just as convinced that what Jesus served was fermented. However, their argument is based upon the assumption that wine always means the fermented grape juice.

To resolve this issue, it will be necessary to study the Mosaic law regarding the Passover Supper, the customs and practices that became a part of the Passover Supper but which were not required by Passover law, teaching of the New Testament about the Lord's Supper, and about our redemption through His blood.

This is a subject that must not be dealt with superficially. I have read every book and paper dealing with the matter that I could purchase, borrow, or study in libraries, and I have not found one that covers all the different aspects at issue.

The sacrament of the Lord's Supper is an ordinance established by the Lord Jesus Himself. We are commanded to perpetuate this rite until He returns. The bread and the fruit of the vine are the appointed elements of the Supper. It is of vital importance to the Church that the full signification of this ordinance be understood. Jesus said, after He had blessed and broken the bread, "This is my body." And He said of that which was in the cup, "This is my blood of the new testament, which is shed for many for the remission of sins."

The Passover law was very specific about what kind of bread should be used. Would the Lord be less particular about the kind of wine that should be used in a sacrament to commemorate the shedding of His blood for the remission of our sins?

It is this writer's firm conviction that the appointed wine for the Communion service is the unfermented, and in the following pages I shall present my reasons for this conviction.

Chapter 25

FERMENTED WINE FORBIDDEN AT THE PASSOVER

When Jesus instituted the Lord's Supper, He and His disciples were eating the Passover, and Passover law would not permit anything fermented on the table or in the house. The fruit of the vine that was in the cup Jesus gave to His disciples to drink, in order to conform to all Passover regulations could not be fermented.

It is admitted that many Jews today use fermented wine at Passover, and Rabbinical authorities are not agreed as to whether Passover wine should be fermented or unfermented. Their disagreement, however, does not prove that Jesus did or did not use fermented wine.

A study of the law of the Passover as given by Moses will reveal, to the amazement of many Bible readers, that neither fermented nor unfermented wine was an essential part of the Passover Supper. Not once in all the law of Moses, where regulations are given for the keeping of Passover, is wine in any state, fermented or unfermented, so much as mentioned as a required part of the Passover.

Passover is also called the Feast of Unleavened Bread. During the seven days of unleavened bread, special offerings and sacrifices were made which included drink offerings, but these were not consumed at the Passover table. They were poured out for "a burnt offering unto the Lord...an offering made by fire unto the Lord" (Lev. 23:4-14; Num. 28:16-25).

In studying the teachings and practices of modern Judaism and Christianity, we must remember that twentieth century practices of Jews or Christians are to be recognized as a guide only as they conform to the Word of God. Traditionalism must never set aside God's Word. The Bible is the final authority. "To the law and to the testimony: if they speak not according to this word, it is because there is no light in them" (Isa. 8:20). This must ever be the standard of the people of God.

Christian Churches today, Protestant, Roman Catholic, Eastern Orthodox, all have traditions and practices that are not Biblical in origin, neither were they observed by the Church of the First Century. It can be similarly said of modern Judaism that many practices of today were not a part of the ordinances and ceremonies that were given to Israel at Mt. Sinai. Whether Protestant, Roman Catholic, Eastern Orthodox, or Jewish, tradition must never be allowed to supersede the Written Word.

If the manner in which the Passover is kept today by Jews conforms to "the law and the testimony" of Moses, then it may help us to determine whether or not fermented wine was used at Passover at the time of Christ. If their observance of Passover does not conform it will be of no help.

A fact too long ignored by writers on both sides of the temperance issue is that Mosaic law did not require either fermented or unfermented wine at Passover. The only items of food which were specified as essential to the supper were the roasted lamb, bitter herbs, and unleavened bread, which more properly should be rendered unfermented. Other foods were neither required nor forbidden. However, if other foods were eaten, they must conform to the law in regard to leaven, or fermentation. They were not forbidden to use wine, but if they did, it must conform and not be leavened, or fermented, and they could keep the Passover without any wine, either fermented or unfermented, and still conform to Mosaic requirements.

After Israel became settled in Caanan, and the kingdom was set up, other customs developed in the keeping of Passover, which were not required by Moses, including the taking of wine. It is not known when this practice began, but it eventually became a part of the Passover observance, so much so that at the time of the Last Supper it was the custom to take the cup four times: first, at the beginning of the meal; second, before the eating of the lamb. The third cup was called the "cup of blessing." The "cup of Hallel," or the "cup of the Hallel," was the fourth cup, although some writers reverse the order of the last two, making the "cup of blessing" the last cup.

The Gospel of Luke, chap. 22, makes it clear that Jesus took the cup two times, and if the current Passover custom was observed may have taken it four times. Paul, in 1 Cor. 10:16 refers to this cup and says, "The cup of blessing which we bless, is it not the communion of the blood of Christ? The bread which we break, is it not the communion of the body of Christ?"

Although it is not certain when the taking of the cup at the Passover began, there is no doubt in my mind that it was divinely ordered that when it came time for the Lord to keep this Supper with His disciples and institute the Christian sacrament, the cup would be ready for the occasion.

Now the question before us is whether the cup contained fermented wine or unfermented. This question must be answered according to the requirements of Passover law. For Jesus said in Matt. 5:17, "Think not that I am come to destroy the law, or the prophets: I am not come to destroy, but to fulfil." Jesus fulfilled the law in every requirement. He was the antitype of which the Passover was the type. So "to the law, and to the prophets." What does the law require concerning things fermented and unfermented?

In studying Jewish laws and customs, it is essential that we keep in mind the difference between Mosaic law and Talmudic law. The law of Moses is contained in the Old Testament, but the Talmud is something quite different. In the Gospels, Jesus at times rebuked the Pharisees for transgressing "the commandment of God by your traditions. . .Thus have ye made the commandment of God of none effect by your tradition. . .teaching for doctrines the commandments of men" (Matt. 15:10). "Then spake Jesus to the multitude, and to his disciples, Saying, The scribes and the Pharisees sit in Moses seat" (Matt. 23:1,2). They had taken the place of Moses and had imposed regulations and customs that were not Mosaic. At other times Jesus said, "Ye say in your law," making a distinction between the law of the scribes and Pharisees and the Law of Moses. Likewise, the Pharisees and scribes accused Jesus and His disciples of transgressing "the traditions of the elders."

Never did Jesus condemn the law of Moses, but referred to it as "the commandment of God." He condemned the "traditions of the elders" when they contradicted the law of God. While the Jews were in Babylon, doctrines, traditions, and laws developed which were handed down orally through the years until finally compiled in written form. These writings are known as the Talmud, which means "instruction, teaching." Some of these doctrines and teachings contravened the law of God found in the writings of Moses, the Psalms and the Prophets.

The Talmud consists of a code of laws called the Mishnah, which was put into writing about 189 A.D., and later writings called the Gemara, which deal with history, commentaries on the law, medicine, astronomy, mathematics, and other subjects. There are two compilations of the Talmud, The Palestinian and the Babylonian. Both contain the Mishnah. The Babylonian Talmud was completed about the 7th century A.D., but the Palestinian Talmud was completed earlier and contains the works of Jewish scholars only up to the beginning of the 5th century. Many Orthodox Jews do not accept the Talmud as equal in authority to the Old Testament.

The Mishnah requires that each person be given four cups of wine during the Passover Supper, but his is Talmudic law and not the law given to Moses at Mt. Sinai, which was sixteen centuries before the Mishna was put in writing. Christian writers make a serious mistake when they refer to Jewish law regarding Passover wine without specifying whether it is Talmudic or Mosaic law. Talmudic law requires wine at Passover. Mosaic Law does not.

If the Mishnah had specified that fermented wine must be used, which it does not, this still could not set aside the law of Moses which does not permit anything that is fermented at the Passover. All ferment was to be removed from the house during the entire seven days of unleavened bread.

The law of the Passover as God gave it to Moses is recorded in Ex. 12. Following is the portion that specifies what foods were to be eaten at the supper. "Speak ye unto all the congregation of Israel, saying, In the tenth day of this month they shall take to them every man a lamb according to the house of their fathers, a lamb for an house: And if the household be too little for the lamb, let him and his neighbour next unto his house take it according to the number of the souls; every man according to his eating shall make your count for the lamb. Your lamb shall be without blemish, a male of the first year: ye shall take it out from the sheep, or from the goats. . . And they shall eat the flesh in that night, roast with fire, and unleavened bread; and with bitter herbs they shall eat it. . .Seven days shall yet eat unleavened bread; even the first day ye shall put away leaven out of your houses: for whosoever eateth leavened bread from the first day until the seventh day, that soul shall be cut off from Israel. . .And ye shall observe the feast of unleavened bread; . . . ye shall eat unleavened bread until the one and twentieth day of the month at even. Seven days shall there be no leaven found in your houses; for whosoever eateth that which is leavened, even that soul shall be cut off from the congregation of Israel, whether he be a stranger, or born in the land. Ye shall eat nothing leavened; in all your habitations shall ye eat unleavened bread."

Only three foods are required here: the roasted lamb, bitter herbs, and unleavened (unfermented) bread. But that is not all that the law required. All ferment and everything fermented had to be removed from the house during the entire seven days. Other foods were not required or prohibited. But if used, they must conform to the law regarding ferment. Jos. 5:10,11 shows that at one time Israel kept the Passover and in addition to the lamb, bitter herbs, and unfermented bread, they ate parched corn, but nowhere in the Old Testament does it mention the taking of wine in any form, fermented or unfermented, at the Passover. Long before the time of Christ it became the customer to take the fruit of the vine at Passover, but Mosaic law did not require it.

Following are all the references in the Old Testament dealing with the Passover. Gen. 12:1-51; 13:3-7; 23:15-18; 34:18-25; Lev. 23:5,6,17; Num. 9:1-14; 28:16,17; 33:3; Deut. 16:3,4; Jos. 5:10,11; 2 Kings 23:21-23; 2 Chr. 8:13; 30:1-27; 35:1-19; Ezra 6:19-22; Eze. 45:21-24; Hos. 7:4; Amos 4:5. Not once in any of these passages is wine mentioned, whether fermented or unfermented.

It is significant that the Passover is called the feast of unleavened bread ten times in these eighteen passages. This term is also used in the New Testament. In the next chapter we shall see that the word ferment is a more proper word than leaven, and unfermented bread is more proper than unleavened bread. And with the requirement of all ferment and all fermented things to be removed from the house, and nothing fermented to be on the table, we would be just as proper in calling it the feast of unfermented things, which would included both solids and liquids.

Jesus is not only our Passover, sacrificed for us, but He is also Lord of the Passover. How can we reconcile the Lord, who established the Passover Supper, and required all ferment to be removed from the house for seven days during this holy season, and forbade eating of anything during the Passover that was fermented, Himself taking that which was fermented, giving it to His disciples to drink, and appointing it for us to take in remembrance of Him who was not permitted to see corruption?

Chapter 26

FERMENTATION THE TRUE MEANING OF LEAVEN

In the preceding chapter we saw that wine was not a required item of food at the Passover supper. It was not forbidden. Neither were other foods forbidden, but anything taken at the Passover had to be without leaven. In this chapter we shall see that the Hebrew words rendered leaven should have been more properly rendered ferment. This was applied to liquids as well as solids, which means that if wine were used at Passover it had to be unfermented.

C.C.M. Douglas defines leaven with the word ferment, and shows that it applies to both solids and liquids: "Leaven is that principle by which the process of fermentation is produced, whether in solid substances like bread, or in fermented liquors. . .Leaven being the principle of fermentation (and it is easy to see how honey was classed with it, since it was to the ancients what sugar is to us), represented the power of change in the direction of decomposition and corruption, and was therefore excluded from the materials out of which an offering by fire for the altar of God might be formed."

This is confirmed by Funk & Wagnalls Desk Standard Dictionary, which says that leaven means, "I. vt. 1. To make light by fermentation. 2. To affect in character; imbue. II. n. 1. fermenting dough, or anything that causes fermentation. 2. Any influence that causes general change. (Latin leve, raise.)"

Webster's Collegiate Dictionary, 5th Edition, "n. (Old French levain, from Latin levamen, alleviation, taken in the sense of a raising, that which raises, from levare to raise.) 1. Any substance used to produce fermentation as in doughs or liquids; especially a portion of fermenting dough reserved for this use; yeast. 2. Sometimes, any ferment. 3. Anything which makes a general assimilating change in a mass or aggregate; as, a leaven of wit. —v.t. 1. To cause to ferment, as dough; hence to make light by a leavening agent. 2. To mingle or permeate with a transforming element or admixture; to imbue, impregnate, alloy, or the like."

New American Encyclopedic Dictionary, Vol. III, "leaven, levain, levein, s. (French levain, from Latin levamen=that which raises: levo=to raise.)

"1. Lit.: A substance used or intended to produce fermentation, as in dough; specifically, a portion of sour dough, which, being mixed with a larger quantity of other dough, causes fermentation, and makes it lighter; yeast, barm. 'For ye shall burn no leaven nor any honey in any offering of the Lord made by fire.'—Leviticus ii. 11.

"2. Fig.: Any mixture which causes or tends to cause a general change in the mass. It generally means something which depraves or corrupts that with which it is mixed. 'Take heed and beware of the leaven of the Pharisees and of the Saducees.'—Matthew xvi. 6.

"leaven, V.T. (LEAVEN, s.) 1. Lit.: to cause or produce fermentation in; to raise and make light, as dough. 2. Fig. to taunt, to corrupt, to deprave, to imbue. . .

"leavened, s. (Eng. leaven; -ed.) 1. Lit.: Fermented."

The meaning of leaven is ferment. This is also the scriptural meaning. Leavened bread was forbidden at Passover because it was fermented bread. But fermented bread was not all that was forbidden. Anything leavened, solid or liquid, was forbidden because it was fermented. It was not permitted in the house during the seven days of the Passover celebration because it was fermented.

The reason for all this is that fermentation is corruption. As the Passover Lamb was a symbol of the Christ who was to give His life for the salvation of the world, even so the bread was a symbol of the body of Him Who said, "I am the bread of life." This will be presented more fully later. As He was not to see corruption, "For thou wilt not leave my soul in hell; neither wilt thou suffer thine Holy One to see corruption" (Ps. 16:10; Acts 2:27), neither could that which was to symbolize Him, His body or His blood have any corruption or ferment in it. For this reason all ferment was removed from the house, and nothing fermented could be on the Passover table.

Even Bullinger, who was not sympathetic with the total abstinence position and held that grape juice was not wine unless it was fermented, in his Companion Bible, admits that the word leaven means ferment. In his marginal reading for Ex. 12:15, 19, 20, where the word leaven appears, he says, "leaven=fermented bread." Bullinger's notes on leaven are all the more important because he cannot be accused of bias toward the total abstinence view.

In Ex. 13:3 & 7 where the word leaven is used, and in Deut. 16:4 where the words leavened bread appear, Bullinger's marginal note in each instance says, "leavened=fermented."

In his marginal notes for the words leaven and honey in Lev. 2:11, he says, "honey. Leaven is fermentation, and honey or sweet liquor is the cause of it. These two things forbidden because there was no error or corruption in the Antitype. All was divine perfection. Nothing therefore which answers to leaven may be in our sacrifice of praise now."

In Appendix 38, in the back of the Companion Bible, leaven is further explained, "Its first occurance in Ex. 12:15 significantly marks it as something to be 'put away.' There is no dispute as to the meaning of the word, which is sour or fermenting dough. The difference lies in its interpretation. This can be gathered only from its usage by the Holy Spirit...Thus in every instance it is associated with, and symbolical of, only that which is evil."

Leaven which is a Latin word literally means to raise. Although dictionaries define it as meaning ferment, still there are leavens which do not ferment or corrupt. Beaten eggs and baking powders cause dough to rise without fermenting or corrupting them. Yeast causes fermentation, whether in dough or in grape juice. For that reason the word ferment is actually more correct and literal as a rendering for the Hebrew words, for they denote a fermentation caused by yeast or barm, not to baking powder or beaten eggs.

Yeast is defined by the New American Encyclopedic Dictionary as, "1. Chemically: Barm. The yellowish, vixoid substance deposited from beer, or which rises to the surface of saccharine solutions during the process of fermentation. . .Yeast is the potent agent in the production of alcohol from sugar, each molecule of sugar splitting up into alcohol and carbonic anhydride, by a process which is not clearly understood. . .Grapejuice, and several other vegetable juices, when left for a few days at a suitable temperature develope yeast cells in great abundance, without any addition of yeast, probably from the presence of spores in the surrounding atmosphere. In breadmaking, yeast, both in its liquid and dried states, is added with warm water to flour to give a start to the fermentation process, thereby supplying the carbonic-acid gas, which communicates a spongy or light texture to the bread. It is also essential to the production of wine from the grape juice and other fruit juices, the manufacture of beer, and the preparation of distilled spirits. . .yeast, vi.i. (YEAST,s.) To ferment."

The same dictionary defines barm as, "The frothy scum which rises to the surface of beer when it is undergoing the process of fermentation, and is used in making bread. The same as YEAST (q.v.)."

At Passover, the Israelites were forbidden to eat any bread made with yeast. It had to be without yeast, unfermented bread. They were also required to put all yeast and everything containing yeast out of the house for seven days. "Seven days ye shall eat unleavened bread; even the first day ye shall put away leaven out of your houses, for whosoever eateth leavened bread from the first day until the seventh day, that soul shall be cut off from Israel. . .And ye shall observe the feast of unleavened bread; . . . ye shall eat unleavened bread, . . . Seven days shall there be no leaven found in your houses: for whosoever eateth that which is leavened, even that soul shall be cut off from the congregation of Israel. . .Ye shall eat nothing leavened" (Ex. 12:8-34). In each of the above usages of leaven the word ferment would have been more literal and proper. The leaven used by the Israelites for making bread was yeast, the same yeast that ferments grape juice and other fruit juices.

The Bible contains five Hebrew words and two Greek words in this connection and all five convey the meaning of ferment.

Seor was what had to be removed from the house and which rendered anything containing it unfit for Passover.

Strong defines seor as, "barm or yeast cake (as swelling by fermentation)." Seor is what causes fermentation in wine, and it is what causes fermentation in bread. The yeast that causes wine to ferment is the same yeast that is used in making bread. In ancient times women would go to the barrels in which wine had fermented, and in their hands would take some of the yeast sediment from the bottom of the barrel and mix it in their bread dough to ferment or leaven the bread. Bread dough will not rise without the addition of yeast. The yeast, ferment, must be added to the dough. The yeast, seor, ferment could be obtained from the sediment in the bottom of the barrel in which grape juice had fermented. During Passover seor could not be kept in the house.

Modern wine makers may add yeast to the grape juice to cause it to ferment faster. Brewers use it in making beer. The action of the yeast, seor, in the dough is that of fermentation, just as it is in the grape juice.

The Hebrew word for unleavened bread is matstsah (matzo) which Strong defines as, "sweet (i.e. not soured or bittered with yeast); specifically an unfermented cake or loaf; or (eliptically) the festival of Passover (because no leaven was then used)."

The Hebrew word chamets according to Strong is, "a primitive root; to be pungent; i.e. in taste (sour, i.e. literally fermented, or figuratively harsh), in color (dazzling)."

Chametz (also hhametz) Strong says is, "from chamets, ferment, (fig.) extortion."

The fifth Hebrew word is mahhmetzeth (also makhmetzet). It is the participle of chametz according to Douglas, and is used "to describe any substance, generally what was used for food, on which seor had acted."

Young defines chamets as, "anything leavened or fermented."

The Greek word zume, according to Strong, means, "ferment (as if boiling up);" and zumoo means "to cause to ferment."

Azumes of course means not fermented, the letter alpha giving zume the negative meaning.

Note particularly how the word ferment is used in the definition of these words. Nothing that was fermented or contained ferment, whether solid or liquid, was to be permitted to remain in the house.

Pixley's arguments for using the words ferment, fermented, unfermented instead of leaven, leavened, unleavened in connection with the Passover are irresistible and should be examined by anyone who questions the propriety of these terms. He has shown that ferment is more proper than leaven.

Chapter 27

FERRAR FENTON AND THE WORD FERMENT

Ferrar Fenton's Translation shows an overwhelming preference for the word ferment. Out of 99 renderings, Fenton uses the words unleavened cakes 2 times, and leavened 2 times. In 95 other renderings, where the King James Version says, leaven, leavened, leaveneth, unleavened, Fenton says unfermented 9 times, unfermented biscuit 1 time, unfermented bread 22 times, unfermented cakes 4 times, unfermented wafers 2 times, ferment 20 times, fermented 10 times, fermenting 1 time, ferments 2 times.

In Exodus 12:8, 15, 17-20, Fenton's Translation reads, "They shall eat it with unfermented bread. . .You shall eat unfermented bread for seven days; that is: in the first day you shall remove ferment from your houses; for all who eat fermented bread, then, that person shall be excommunicated from Israel. . .Therefore guard these days of unfermented bread. . .beginning at the fourteenth day of the month at the dusk to eat unfermented bread. . . During seven days, ferment shall not be brought into your houses; for everyone eating of fermented bread, that person shall be excommunicated from the families of Israel. . .You shall eat biscuits."

Ex. 12:34, 39, "So the people took up the dough before it was fermented with yeast, rolled up in their knapsacks on their shoulders. . .They also baked the dough which they had brought from the Mitseraim into biscuits, before it was fermented, for the Mitserites drove them, and they were not able to ferment it, as well as also being ordered not to do it."

Ex. 13:3, 6, 7, ". . .so you shall not eat fermented bread. . .For seven days you shall eat biscuits. . .You shall eat biscuits for seven days, and fermented bread shall not be seen with you; nor shall ferment be seen in all your boundaries."

Lev. 23:6, "And on the fifteenth day of that month is the Feast of unfermented bread to the EVER-LIVING. For seven days you shall eat unfermented bread."

Fenton uses the word ferment in the New Testament also, and in two places the word yeast. Matt. 13:35, "The Kingdom of Heaven is like yeast, which a woman took and mixed in three stones of flour, so that the whole was fermented by it." Matt. 16:6 & 12, "Jesus then addressing them, said, 'Look out, and take care to keep free from the ferment of the Pharisees and Saducees.' . . .They then fully comprehend that He had not told them to guard against the ferment of the bread of the Pharisees and Sadducees, but to avoid their teaching." Mark 8:15, "And he warned them, saying, "Take care! beware of the ferment of the Pharisees, and of the ferment of Herod.'" Luke 12:1, "He began to say to His disciples: 'Guard yourselves from the ferment of the Pharisees.'" Luke 13:20, 21: "Again He said, 'To what shall I liken the Kingdom of God? It is like yeast, which a woman took, and mixed in three measures of flour, until the whole was fermented.'" 1 Cor. 5:6-8, "Your pride is not noble. Do you not know that a little ferment ferments the whole mass? Clean out the old ferment, so that you may be a fresh mass, and thus you will unfermented. For Christ your passover is sacrificed for us, that we may keep a festival: not with an old ferment, neither in a ferment of filth, and wickedness: but, on the contrary, with unfermented purity and truth." Galatians 5:9, "A little ferment ferments the whole mass."

Fenton considered the word ferment to be more proper in expressing the meaning of the Hebrew Greek words which other translators render leaven.

Fenton's use of the word ferment makes it clear that nothing that was fermented, either solids or liquids, was used at the Passover and nothing fermented, either solids or liquids, should be used at the communion table for Christians.

This writer is unable to harmonize Jesus, the Lord of the Passover, and our Passover Lamb, forbidding the use of fermented solids at Passover, but permitting the use of fermented liquids at Passover, and when partaking of the Passover with His disciples observing the law which forbade fermented solids, but serving fermented liquids to His disciples, especially when the law required that all ferment must be removed from the house during the entire seven days.

Chapter 28

THE NEW WORLD TRANSLATION AND THE WORD FERMENT

That the word ferment more accurately carries the meaning of the Hebrew and Greek than leaven was recognized in the original New World Translation of the Holy Scriptures published at first in five volumes from 1953 to 1960, and bound together in one volume in 1963, by Watchtower Bible and Tract Society of New York, Inc. (Also International Bible Students Association). These two organizations publish the literature of Jehovah's Witnesses.

In Exodus 12 and 13, this translation uses such words as: unfermented cakes, fermentation, what is fermented, no fermentation, unfermented bread, it had not fermented. In Lev. 2:11 the expressions a fermented thing, no fermentation are used. Anything fermented is used in Lev. 6:17; unfermented in Lev. 10:12. Yeast and fermented is used in Matt. 13:33. Yeast, ferments, ferment, unfermented in 1 Cor. 5:6, 7. And in other references these words are used showing that the translators felt that ferment was more accurate than leaven.

Now the use of yeast and ferment by the translators was correct. However this was not in harmony with the doctrine and practice of Jehovah's Witnesses. They believe that Bible wine is fermented; they use fermented wine in their communion service, and also in their homes. This put them in a dilemma.

In 1961, a much smaller revision of the New World Translation, which does not contain the marginal references and footnotes of the first translation, was published in which the revisors made some changes which were more in keeping with their position that sanctions the use of fermented wine.

In Ex. 12:15, the original translation requires fermentation to be taken from the houses, which would include both solids and liquids. The words sour dough were substituted. This would require only solids with fermentation to be removed. In the 19th verse, in the original translation, no fermentation was to be found in their houses, which would apply to both solids and liquids. Again the words sour dough were substituted, which would require only fermented solids to be removed. In the same verse the original translation stated that anyone so much as tasting that which was fermented was to be cut off from the assembly of Israel. The revisors used the words, what is leavened. In Ex. 13:7, which, according to the first rendering, required that nothing fermented was to be seen with them, and no fermentation was to be permitted in all their boundaries, the revisors changed to nothing leavened and no sour dough. Nothing fermented and no fermentation would apply to

93

wine as well as bread. We think only of bread and cakes as being leavened, and do not use the expression leavened wine.

Most of the doctrines of Jehovah's Witnesses are un-Biblical, but their original translation of these passages dealing with our subject was proper, and in their revision where they made no changes in such passages they are still correct.

I cannot approve of compromising the Scriptures to make them conform to doctrine. We must make our doctrine conform to the Scriptures.

Chapter 29

YOUNG'S LITERAL TRANSLATION AND ANYTHING FERMENTED

Dr. Young, who gave us Young's Analytical Concordance, is also the author of Young's Literal Translation of the Bible. His translation also confirms our position that nothing fermented was to be a part of the Passover supper.

Ex. 12:14, ". . .for anyone eating anything fermented from the first day till the seventh day, even that person hath been cut off from Israel." Verse 19, ". . . for any one eating anything fermented—that person hath been cut off from the company of Israel, among the sojourners or among the natives of the land; anything fermented ye do not eat, in all your dwellings ye do eat unleavened things." Ex. 13:3, ". . .and anything fermented is not eaten." Verse 6, ". . .unleavened things are not eaten the seven days, and any thing fermented is not seen with thee; yea, leaven is not seen with thee in all they border."

Young uses the words leavened and fermented interchangeably, which he could not do if fermented did not have the same meaning the Hebrew word had. Fermented as I have already shown is a more exact rendering than leavened.

It should be stated here that the Hebrew word for bread is lekhem (lechem), and this word does not appear once in the twelfth and thirteenth chapters of Exodus. The Hebrew word matstsah (matzo) does appear, and this is a biscuit, cake, cracker that is flat, has not risen in the baking because it has no ferment in it. This is what the Israelites were told to eat during Passover. That which was forbidden, and had to be removed from the house during the seven days was chamets and seor. The seor was what caused the fermentation, and the chamets was that which the seor had acted upon and caused it to be fermented. The seor which caused the bread dough to ferment was the same which caused the wine to ferment.

Chapter 30

WHAT THE PASSOVER LAW SPECIFICALLY REQUIRED

The law of the Passover was specific. It required eating of the roasted lamb, bitter herbs and unfermented bread, and removal from the house for seven days all ferment and everything that was fermented.

It did not require the taking of any other food, either solid or liquid. Neither did the law forbid other foods. However, if other foods were taken they must conform to the requirement that they contain no ferment, whether solids or liquids.

The juice of the grape was not required by the law of Moses, neither was it forbidden. It could be used, but if used it must not be fermented. Use of fermented wine at the Passover would be a violation of Mosaic law, regardless of what Talmudic law said one way or the other.

Jesus did not and could not use fermented wine when He and His disciples observed the last Passover Supper and instituted the Christian ordinance of the Lord's Supper. Jesus never violated any of the laws of God. He kept them and fulfilled them. He said of Himself, "Think not that I am come to destroy the law, or the prophets: I am not come to destroy, but to fulfil" (Matt. 5:17).

The taking of wine at the Passover did become a custom to such an extent that by the time Jesus and His disciples observed the Passover the cup was taken four times. Luke 22 mentions the Lord taking the cup twice during the Last Supper, at the beginning and at the end. Luke does not say that He took it four times, although He could have done so in fulfillment of Jewish custom.

The taking of the cup at Passover became so established that it eventually became regarded as a requirement, and the Mishna, which was put into writing 189 A.D., required everyone to be given four cups. But we must remember that this was not a part of the law of Moses. The Mishna was "the tradition of the elders" which became regarded as law, but that which Moses commanded was the law of God, given at Mt. Sinai.

Regardless of what the Mishna might require, the law of Moses stands supreme. If the Mishna contravened the law of the Lord, it must be disregarded. "To the law and to the testimony: if they speak not according to this word, it is because there is no light in them" (Isa. 8:20).

Let us also remember that, even though the Mishna did require taking the cup four times, it did not require the cup to contain fermented wine. Had the Mishna required fermented wine, there would be no disagreement today among Talmudic Jews as to whether Passover wine should be fermented or unfermented.

97

Chapter 31

TESTIMONY OF JEWISH AUTHORITIES ON PASSOVER WINE

Three positions are taken by Jewish scholars on Passover wine. 1. Some say that only fermented wine should be used. 2. Others say unfermented wine should be used. 3. Still others say that either fermented or unfermented wine may be used.

This writer concedes that some say fermented wine should be used, and it is not necessary to give their reasons here. We are interested in what those who use unfermented wine say.

Encyclopedia Britannica, 8th Edition, published in 1859, Vol. xvii, p. 333, subject Passover, says: "Wine also to the quantity of four or five cups was drunk by each person. Considerable dispute has been raised as to whether the wine used on this occasion was fermented or unfermented,—was the ordinary wine, in short, or the pure juice of the grape. Those who hold it was unfermented appeal mainly to the expression 'unfermented things,' which is the true rendering of the word translated 'unleavened bread.' The rabbins would seem to have interpreted the command respecting ferment as extending to the wine as well as to the bread of the passover. The modern Jews, accordingly, generally use raisin wine, after the injunction of the rabbins."

The Universal Jewish Encyclopedia, subject wine, says, "During the prohibition period in the United States (1920-1933) the federal government permitted the manufacture and sale of wine for sacramental purposes. Conservative as well as Reformed rabbis in the country maintained that as far as the Jewish ritual was concerned there was no need of this special privilege, since grape juice could be used instead of wine. Louis Ginzberg, in his monograph on the subject (1922), justified this position through an exhaustive research in Talmudic law and later rabbinic decisions. Strictly orthodox rabbis generally insisted on the uses of wine. Charles A. Rubenstein."

The Jewish Encyclopedia, subject wine, says, "According to Raba, one may squeeze the juice of a bunch of grapes into a cup and say the 'Kiddush' (B.B.97b.)."

Writting on Passover Wine in the Encyclopedia of Temperance and Prohibition, G.W. Samson gave the following, "Though studious efforts have been made to draw from non-conforming Rabbis statements that the wines of their Passover are now and have ever been intoxicating, the following statement of Judge Joachimsen (so long and highly esteemed in New York and lately deceased) has not only not been contravened but has been confirmed by even the most liberal Rabbis. In response to a request for a written statement of a former verbal declaration the following note was received by the writer of this article: '336 East 69th Street, New York, Feb. 15, 1881. —Rev. and Dear Sir: In answer to your favor of yesterday's date, I repeat that the great majorities of conforming Jews in this city use wine made from raisins at the Passover Feast. Of course the raisins are fresh. Such raisin wine is used in all conforming synagogues for the sanctification of the Sabbath and holy days, i.e. for Kiddush and also for services as circumcisions and weddings. Some, but not many, people use imported wine — Italian, Hungarian or German — which is certified as 'Pesach' or 'Kosher wine.' I am most truly yours, P.J. Joachimsen.'

"It thus appears that the wines used by all conforming Jews are free from ferment, and Judge Joachimsen in a subsequent note refers to synagogues of New York City Jews from 'Tangiers, Morocco, Tunis' on the African coast; from 'Gibraltar, Spain, and Portugal;' also 'French, Hollandish, English, German, Russian and Bohemian, Polish and Lithuanian,' — all conforming synagogues."

We need to comment here that the English word raisin means dried grapes. This is not the meaning of the same word in the French language. In French the same word means the grape itself, fresh, not dried. A cluster of grapes in French would be a cluster of raisins.

Two customs have been perpetuated among Jews in making unfermented wine for ceremonial purposes. One custom is to squeeze the fresh juice from the grapes immediately before the ceremony or at the time of the ceremony into a cup, as the cupbearer did for Pharaoh in the time of Joseph. Of course this is not what Jesus and His disciples did when they observed Passover, for the harvest of grapes had been about seven months before and they would not have fresh grapes on hand. They would have on hand both the dried grapes (raisins) and preserved juices in various forms.

The other custom which they could have used is to put chopped raisins (dried grapes) in an earthen vessel, add water and let them simmer in an oven or on the stove for a time. Then the skins are removed and the juice put into vessels for use during the Passover ceremony. Some families would even have hot water on hand to be used right at the supper to kill any ferment that may have developed in the juice. This is what Britannica and Judge Joachimsen referred to when they spoke of using raisin wine. Of course others would use the grape juice that was preserved unfermented in various forms, and still others use fermented wine.

There are raisin wines on the market which are fermented, but this is not the raisin wine we refer to above which was prepared carefully so that no ferment would be in it.

As I write this chapter it is just seven days until the Jewish Passover, which, this year, comes on the Thursday before the Christian's Good Friday. I live in Royal Oak, one of the northern suburbs of the Detroit area. The city of Oak Park, close to Royal Oak, has a large Jewish population, and the supermarkets in Oak Park during this season are well stocked with Kosher foods for the Passover season.

Included in the items of food for Passover, I found four different brands of Kosher grape juice, one brand being imported from Israel. Two different kinds of grape juice were offered under each brand name, the Concord grape juice or the Muscat grape juice. On the label of each bottle were the words in English and in Hebrew, "Kosher for Passover." These grape juices were unfermented. But they were prepared especially for Passover.

I have talked to numerous Jews about this grape juice and have been told that many Jews today use this grape juice at Passover instead of fermented wine. And why not? It conforms to Mosaic Passover law. Fermented wine does not.

On the label around the bottle of one of the brands of grape juice I found this statement, "Produced under strict Orthodox Rabbinical supervision of the Union of Orthodox Jewish Congregations of America."

Not long ago, I stepped into a store in Oak Park, specializing in Hebrew Bibles, books and literature dealing with the history and matters of interest to the Jews, and other religious items used by Jews in their homes and Synagogues.

The owner and operator of the store was standing behind the counter, a dignified elderly Rabbi with a grey beard and wearing the customary head covering worn by Jews in their Synagogues and Temples.

I introduced myself as a minister, stating that I was seeking some information regarding the Passover, and then asked if it were the practice among some Jews to use unfermented grape juice at Passover instead of fermented wine.

The Rabbi's immediate answer was, "Grape juice? Yah!"

My older daughter has eaten the Passover Supper with three different families. Two of these families had unfermented grape juice for the ones who did not take fermented wine. She was told that some Jewish families mix the grape juice with soda water to make it more brisk in taste. And the supermarkets I visited carried soda water for this purpose, and it too was marked Kosher.

The statement that all Jews use fermented wine at the Passover, and therefore Jesus also used it at the Last Supper, is contrary to the facts.

It was the purpose of this chapter to show from competent Jewish testimony and practice that, according to Jewish law, and present day practice the use of unfermented grape juice at Passover is permissible, it is done, and it violates no Passover requirements. All this has been shown.

It is admitted that fermented wine is used at Passover by many Jews, and different brands of wine with varying percentages of alcohol are available and the words "Kosher for Passover" are on the labels. But the point is that unfermented wine meets all Passover requirements. In fact, the fermented does not, for Moses required all ferment to be removed from the house for seven days.

It is established that unfermented wine is used at Passover. If the advocates of fermented wine reply that this was not always so, and the use of the unfermented was not customary in the time of Christ, but was permitted later, they are placed in the dilemma of answering three questions.

First, what proof do they have that unfermented wine was not used in the time of Christ at the Passover? Second, at what time in subsequent history did the use of unfermented wine become permissible and an established custom among Jews? Third, what was the reason for permitting unfermented wine and by what or whose authority was the permission given?

Now, if unfermented wine is used at Passover, and was used in the time of Christ at Passover, why should Christians use fermented wine at the Lord's Table?

Chapter 32

THE INCORRUPTIBLE BLOOD OF CHRIST

It is a belief of all evangelical Churches that the Passover Lamb served as a type of Christ. Paul wrote in 1 Cor. 5:7, "For even Christ our passover is sacrificed for us." Jesus is the Great Antitype. All types and symbols of the Old Testament Passover were to be fulfilled in Him.

Luke 22:19, 20 says, "And he took bread, and gave thanks, and brake it, and gave unto them, saying, This is my body which is given for you: this do in remembrance of me. Likewise also the cup after the supper, saying, This cup is the new testament (covenant) in my blood, which is shed for you." The unfermented bread in this Passover Supper served as the body of Christ which was broken for us, and the cup served as His blood which was shed for us.

Jesus had said previously in John 6:48-58, "I am the bread of life. Your fathers did eat manna in the wilderness, and are dead. This is the bread which cometh down from heaven, that a man may eat thereof, and not die. I am the living bread which came down from heaven: if any man eat of this bread, he shall live for ever: and the bread that I will give is my flesh, which I will give for the life of the world. . .Verily, verily, I say unto you, Except ye eat the flesh of the Son of man, and drink his blood, ye have no life in you. Whoso eateth my flesh, and drinketh my blood, hath eternal life; and I will raise him up at the last day. For my flesh is meat indeed, and my blood is drink indeed. He that eateth my flesh, and drinketh my blood, dwelleth in me, and I in him. As the living Father hath sent me, and I live by the Father: so he that eateth me, even he shall live by me. This is that bread which came down from heaven; not as your fathers did eat manna, and are dead: he that eateth of this bread shall live forever."

Here Jesus speaks of eating his flesh and drinking his blood. Then on the night of the Last Supper, Jesus took the cup and said, "This cup is the new testament (covenant) in my blood," and they all drank of that cup. He also took the bread, and broke it, and said, "This is my body which is given for you," and they all ate of the broken bread.

To fully conform to the Mosaic law of the Passover, both the bread and that which was in the cup had to be unfermented. It is just as reasonable to assume that Jesus used fermented bread as it is to assume that He used fermented wine at this Passover.

Paul writing about ferment and about Christ being our Passover, said in 1 Cor. 5:7, 8, "Do you not know that a little ferment ferments the whole mass? Clean out the old ferment, so that you may be a fresh mass, and thus you will be unfermented. For even Christ our passover is sacrificed for us, that we may keep a festival; not with an old ferment, neither in a ferment of filth and wickedness; but, on the contrary with unfermented purity and truth." I have used Ferrar Fenton's Translation here for it is more exact than our common version. Note particularly that "Christ our passover is sacrificed for us."

To conform to all Passover requirements, both the bread and that which was in the cup had to be unfermented. Now the body and blood of the Lord were without corruption. Psalm 16:10, speaking prophetically of Christ, says, "Thou wilt not leave my soul in hell; neither wilt thou suffer thine Holy One to see corruption." Peter quoted this on the Day of Pentecost (Acts 2:27), applying it to the resurrected Lord. The process of corruption did not work on either the body or blood of Jesus.

We are told in 1 Peter 1:18, 19, "Forasmuch as ye know that ye were not redeemed with corruptible things, as silver and gold, from your vain conversation received by tradition from your fathers; But with the precious blood of Christ, as of a lamb without blemish and without spot. If we were not redeemed with "corruptible things," and if we were redeemed with "the precious blood of Christ," then the blood of Christ had to be uncorrupted and incorruptible.

How could corrupt wine properly symbolize the incorruptible blood of Christ? Fermented wine is corrupt wine, grape juice that has spoiled. My mother would can fruits in the fall, peaches, pears, and grape juice, for the winter. After some days she would go to the basement and look over the jars. Occasionally she would see a jar that had little gas bubbles in it. She would say, "Oh, this is spoiled." What had happened? The juice had fermented, had become corrupted. Fermentation is the process of corruption. Unfermented grape juice is not corrupted.

Which would more properly symbolize the uncorrupted blood of Christ, the fermented or unfermented wine? If unfermented bread was required to properly typify His body that was not permitted to see corruption, how could corrupt, fermented wine be used to properly typify His incorruptible blood? Would not unfermented wine, which has not seen corruption, be much more proper as a type of His incorruptible blood which was shed to save the world from the corruption of sin? It is this writer's firm conviction that, to properly typify the incorruptible blood of our Lord, communion wine must be without corruption, without ferment.

That which causes grape juice to become corrupt is ferment. For the Lord, when He was establishing the New Covenant at this Passover Supper, to use that which was corrupted, fermented wine, to signify His own incorruptible blood, would have been inconsistent and unthinkable.

Paul instructed the Corinthians to put away ferment. Let us read it again as it is in the King James Version, with the exact and literal meaning of the Greek word in parenthesis. "1 Cor. 5:6-8, "Know ye not that a little leaven (ferment), leaveneth (fermenteth) the whole lump? Purge out therefore the old leaven (ferment), that ye may be a new lump, as ye are unleavened (unfermented). For even Christ our Passover is sacrificed for us: Therefore let us keep the feast, not with old leaven (ferment), neither with the leaven (ferment) of malice and wickedness; but with the unleavened (unfermented) bread of sincerity and truth."

Paul was writing here about keeping feast. Fenton uses the word festival. What festival? The festival of the Lord's Supper. Paul uses the word neither here, which tells us that he is referring to two kinds of ferment. As we come to the table of the Lord's Supper, we are to purge out the old ferment, not use it. We are to keep this feast, festival, not with old ferment, nothing fermented. Neither are we to have in our hearts the ferment of malice and wickedness. Nothing fermented on the table, neither are we to have any ferment in our hearts. The King James Version says we are to keep the feast "with the unleavened bread of sincerity and truth." But the word for bread in the Greek is not in the text. Fenton renders it literally, "with unfermented purity and truth."

The table should not have any ferment, either solid or liquid, and as we partake we should do so with unfermented purity and truth.

The word bread was supplied by the translators. The Concordant Version in its interlinear rendering says, "but IN UN-FERMENTEDS OF-sincerety AND TRUTH," which confirms Fenton's rendering.

As in the Old Testament Passover Supper, all ferment was removed from the table and house, even so in the New Testament we are told that all ferment should be removed from the Lord's Table, and also from the heart of the communicant.

Could Paul require the keeping of this Supper without ferment, if the Lord Himself used and permitted ferment?

Chapter 33

DID THE CORINTHIANS GET DRUNK ON COMMUNION WINE?

This writer's position on Communion wine was recently challenged by a minister who wrote asking, "How could the Corinthians get drunk on Communion wine if it were not fermented?" He cited 1 Cor. 11:17-22 as his proof of their getting drunk on sacramental wine. My correspondent apparently felt he had scored a victory on this point for unfermented grape juice would not cause intoxication.

If the preacher had carefully studied the very text he cited, he would have seen the error of his position. "Now in this that I declare unto you I praise you not, that ye come together, not for the better, but for the worse. For first of all, when ye come together in the church, I hear that there be divisions among you; and I partly believe it. For there must be also heresies among you, that they which are approved may be made manifest among you. When ye come together therefore unto one place, this is not to eat the Lord's supper. For in eating every one taketh before his own supper and one is hungry, and another is drunken. What? have ye not houses to eat and drink in? or despise ye the church of God, and shame them that have not? What shall I say to you? shall I praise you in this? I praise you not."

The New Version rendering in Benjamin Wilson's Emphatic Diaglott reads, "But in noticing this matter, That you come together not for the BETTER, but for the worse, I do not praise you. For indeed, in the first place, I hear that on your coming together in the ASSEMBLY, there are divisions among you; and, as to a certain part I believe it; for it is necessary that there should be Factions among you, so that the APPROVED, may be apparent among you. Then, again, your coming together to the SAME place, is not to eat the Lord's Supper; for each one takes first his own Supper at the MEAL; and one, indeed is hungry; and another is satisfied. Have you not Houses in which to EAT and drink? or do you despise the CONGREGATION of GOD, and put the shame THOSE who are POOR? What shall I say to you? Shall I praise you? In this I praise you not." In his Interlinear Literal English rendering of verse 21, Wilson says, "and one is indeed hungry, one but is filled."

The New World Translation original rendering of this phrase says, "so that one is hungry but another is sufficiently fed."

Ferrar Fenton says, "for each one prepares his own individual meal to eat alone; and one may be hungry, another, again, gorged."

Now what were the circumstances? It was the practice among early Christians to have their love feasts (Greek agapae, charitates), in which the entire assembly would participate. No doubt the custom originated at Jeru-

107

salem where the first Christians sold their lands and houses, gave the proceeds to the Apostles, and had all things in common, meals included. These love feasts were carried to other churches in the times of the Apostles and were perpetuated after the Apostles for many years.

The Love Feast was not the same as the Lord's Supper. It was separate from and was followed by the Lord's Supper. "When ye come together into one place, this is not to eat the Lord's supper."

A situation developed at Corinth which Paul felt should be corrected. So he wrote them about what was taking place, not at the Lord's Supper, but in their Love Feasts.

At the Love Feast, all the members who were able to do so brought food which should have been all put together so that every member could partake of it, including the poor ones who were not able to bring anything. In this manner all would be fed and no one would go hungry. This was not being done by all the members at Corinth.

Divisions had developed in the church, and the members would gather in little groups, schisms or heresies, for that is the meaning of the Greek word here, and instead of putting all their food together, some would eat their own meals separately, ignoring the rest, and the poorer members who could not contribute to the meal were humiliated, put to shame, and went hungry. Others were feasting to the full on what they had brought. Paul wrote to correct this.

Many scholars say that the Greek, which is rendered in the King James Version, "another is drunken," does not mean intoxication here. The word is used elsewhere in the Greek New Testament, and in the Greek Septuagint of the Old Testament, where it means to be filled or satisfied. This is the sense in which it is rendered in the translations quoted above.

Benjamin Wilson renders it "satisfied" in the New Version of his Emphatic Diaglott and "filled" in the Interlinear Translation. Then he gives a footnote which says, "Or, is filled to the full; for the word methuein does not necessarily mean drunken, see note on John 2:10."

John 2:10 tells of Jesus turning water into wine at the wedding feast in Cana, and the governor of the feast said to the bridegroom, "Every man at the beginning doth set forth good wine; and when men have well drunk, then that which is worse: but thou hast kept the good wine until now."

Wilson's note on this says, "The Greek expression here does not imply the least degree of intoxication. The verbs, methusko and methuo, from methu, wine, which, from meta thusin, to drink after sacrificing, signify not to inebriate, but to take wine, to drink enough, and in this sense the verb is evidently used in the Septuagint, Gen. xliii. 34; Cant. v. 1; 1 Mac. xvi. 16; Ecclus. 1. 16. And the prophet Isaiah, chap. lviii. 11, speaking of the abundant blessings of the godly compares them to a well-watered garden, which the LXX translates oos keepos methuoon, by which is certainly understood, not a garden drowned with water, but one sufficiently saturated with it, not having one drop too much, nor too little.—Clarke."

This is the sense in which Joseph Benson's Commentary also deals with the expression "another is drunken" in 1 Cor. 11:21. Benson says, "And one is hungry and another is drunken—Or rather, is filled, or plentifully fed, as methuein signifies here, being opposed to one who is hungry. The word used in this sense by the LXX.; Psa. xxv. 9; Jer. xxxviii. 14; John ii. 10, where it is rendered in our translation, when men have well drunk, though it may sometimes signify to drink to excess, yet frequently in Scripture, and sometimes in other writings, denotes no more than to drink sufficiently or to satisfaction: and it would be very unjust to suppose it implies here, that these guests had already transgressed the rules of intemperance. None can seriously imagine the evangelist to be so destitute of common sense as to represent Christ as displaying his glory by miraculously furnishing the company with wine to prolong a drunken revel."

Samson writes, "The Greek verb 'methuo,' found seven times (Matt. 24:49; John 2:10; Acts 2:15; 1 Cor. 11:21; 1 Thes. 5:7; Rev. 17:2, 6), means 'surfeit,' not drunken, as does the noun 'methusma' in the Greek translation of Hos. 4:11; the contrast in 1 Cor. 11:21 being with 'hungry,' and clearly relating to food, not to articles of drink."

Dr. Adam Clarke, in his commentary on 1 Cor. 11:21, says, "The people came together, and it appears brought their provisions with them; some had much, others had less; some ate to excess, others had scarcely enough to suffice nature. 'One was hungry, and the other was drunken, methuei, was filled to the full;' this is the sense of the word in many places of Scripture."

Even if we assume for the moment that the expression does mean that some were getting drunk, we still emphasize the point that they were not getting drunk at the Lord's Supper. What Paul was correcting was a condition that had developed at the Love Feast where some, instead of sharing with others, ate what they had brought by themselves, and if they were drunk, it was because they had brought their own fermented wine and had drunk it to the point of intoxication. It is evident that they did not share it with the poor, for the text says they went without.

The Lord's Supper followed the Love Feast. If these communicants were getting drunk on communion wine, why is it that only some were getting drunk, when all the members were to partake of the communion? When the cup was being taken during the sacrament, I cannot imagine any, during that sacred moment, drinking a sufficient quantity to produce intoxication. Paul was not reproving the Corinthians for getting drunk during the sacrament. He was correcting a situation that had developed during the Love Feast in which some would go hungry while others filled themselves to the full.

Again assuming that the Corinthians had been using fermented wine at the communion, Paul's instructions in the fifth chapter of this Epistle would end the use of fermented wine, and also confirm our position that only the unfermented wine was proper for the Lord's Supper. His instructions were that all old ferment was to be purged from the feast, and this would prevent a recurrence of intoxication. And of course, Paul's instruction here can be no comfort to those who insist on the use of fermented wine for the sacrament.

"Know ye not that little ferment, fermenteth the whole lump? Purge out therefore the old ferment, that ye may be a new lump, as ye are unfermented.

For even Christ our passover is sacrificed for us: Therefore let us keep the feast, not with old ferment, neither with the ferment of malice and wickedness; but with the unfermented sincerity and truth."

A study of the context shows that Paul is especially dealing with a member who was guilty of fornication. To permit him to remain in the assembly would ferment or corrupt the whole church (verses 6-8). So they were to put the sinful member out, and not keep company with him, at least until he made proper amendment in his life. Paul's second Epistle shows that he did make amends.

In giving these instructions, Paul is alluding to the feast of the Passover when all ferment had to be removed from the house and he tells them that as they kept the Lord's Supper they must do the same. The sinning member was a ferment that must be removed or he would ferment the whole church. The Apostle draws an analogy from the Passover Supper here and says, "For even Christ our passover is sacrificed for us." The Lord's Supper was taking the place of the Passover Supper and Paul says, "Therefore, let us keep the feast, not with old ferment, neither with the ferment of malice and wickedness; but with the unfermented of sincerity and truth."

Although he is especially dealing with the matter of handling the sinning member, his allusion to the Passover is meaningless, and the analogy breaks down completely if ferment had been used at the Passover Supper, or if ferment were permitted at the Christian sacrament of the Lord's Supper. "Therefore let us keep the feast not with old ferment,. . .but with the unfermented."

The reproof in chapter 11:21 was relating to something taking place at the Love Feast, which was separate from and was followed by the Lord's Supper. Paul's injunctions in both chapters 5 and 11 would correct any abuse, whether caused by some members drinking fermented wine to inebriety, or eating to the full while others went hungry.

Would it not be inconsistent for Paul to forbid the use of ferment at the Love Feast and permit its use at the Lord's Supper? No one was getting intoxicated on fermented wine served at the Lord's Supper, but even if they were, compliance with Paul's injunction would correct this.

As the Second Epistle to the Corinthians shows that they did as he enjoined them concerning the sinning member, we have no reason to assume that they ignored both the law of the Passover and Paul's admonition concerning ferment at either the Love Feast or the Lord's Supper.

Chapter 34

JESUS TOOK THE CUP

In all four accounts of the Last Supper, not once is the word wine used in the King James Version. Neither is the Greek word for wine found in the Greek text. The significance of this must not be ignored.

This writer firmly believes in the verbal inspiration of the Scriptures, that every word in the original manuscripts was divinely inspired.

In reading the accounts of the Last Supper we find the words cup and fruit of the vine. The Greek word for cup is poterion, and for fruit of the vine is gennematos tes ampelou. The Greek words for wine, oinos and gleukos, are not to be found.

Matt. 26:26-29, "And he took the cup (poterion), and gave thanks, and gave it to them saying, Drink ye all of it; For this is my blood of the new testament, which is shed for many for the remission of sins. But I say unto you, I will not drink henceforth of this fruit of the vine (gennematos tes ampelou), until the day when I drink it new with you in my Father's kingdom."

Mark 14:23-25, "And he took the cup (poterion), and when he had given thanks, he gave it to them: and they all drank of it. And he said unto them, This is my blood of the new testament, which is shed for many. Verily I say unto you, I will drink no more of the fruit of the vine (gennematos tes ampelou), until that day that I drink it new in the kingdom of God."

Luke 22:17-20: "And he took the cup (poterion), and gave thanks, and said, Take this, and divide it among yourselves, For I say unto you, I will not drink of the fruit of the vine (gennematos tes ampelou), until the kingdom of God shall come, And he took the bread, and gave thanks, and brake it, and gave unto them, saying, This is my body which is given for you: This do in remembrance of me. Likewise also the cup (poterion) after supper saying, This cup (poterion) is the new testament in my blood, which is shed for you."

1 Cor. 11:23-28, "After the same manner also he took the cup (poterion), when he had supped, saying, This cup (poterion) is the new testament in my blood: this do ye, as oft as ye drink it, in remembrance of me. For as often as ye eat this bread, and drink this cup (poterion), ye do shew the Lord's death till he come. Wherefore whosoever shall eat this bread, and drink this cup (poterion) of the Lord unworthily, shall be guilty of the body and blood of the Lord. But let a man examine himself, and so let him eat of that bread, and drink of that cup (poterion)."

In these four accounts, the words "fruit of the vine" (gennematos tes ampelou) are used three times, and the word "cup" (poterion) is used ten times. If the Lord had wanted us to understand that fermented wine was used at this supper, why did He not use oinos instead of poterion and

111

gennematos tes ampelou? One who believes in the verbal inspiration of the Scriptures is faced with a verbal difficulty unless he recognizes that these two expressions were inspired of the Lord for a specific reason, and that they had been in common use by the Israelites to denote the freshly expressed grape juice, the preserved grape juice, or the grape itself. It does not mean fermented wine.

Gennematos tes ampelou literally means product of the vine, and it must not have in it that which is not produced by the vine itself. Fermented wine is not the product of the vine. It is the product of corruption, of spoilation. It has constituents that are not produced by the vine, and are not found in the grape. It is also lacking in constituents that are produced by the vine and are found in the grape itself and also in the unfermented grape juice. The grape juice, freshly expressed, may be as much as 30 percent sugar, and some grapes may have more than that at times, but it contains no alcohol. Fermented wine has practically all of the sugar destroyed and may be as much as 14 percent alcohol. The sugar is changed into alcohol and carbon dioxide in the process of corruption which we call fermentation. To say that fermented wine is the product of the vine is like saying that a chocolate malted milk is the product of the cow. To be sure, milk comes from the cow, but a chocolate malted milk has ingredients not found in the fresh milk. They are added in preparing the milk shake.

Similarly, fermented wine contains ingredients that do not come from the vine. After the grape has been removed from the vine and has gone through the winepress, and the juice has been permitted to set several weeks and ferment, that juice is no longer the same juice that was freshly pressed from the grape. When freshly expressed, from 14 to 30 percent of that juice was sugar, the percentages of sugar varying according to the different brands, and the climate in which the grapes were grown. After fermentation a change has taken place. The juice is not the same. The yeast germs have eaten the sugar and excreted carbon dioxide, which is lost in the air, and alcohol which will vary from 7 to 14 percent of the wine, according to the percentage of sugar before fermentation.

The Lord certainly knew how different fermented wine is from the original fruit of the vine, and He knew more than any man about the demoralizing effects of alcohol. Speaking through Solomon in Prov. 20:1, He condemned fermented wine as a mocker, as something that is raging, a deceiver, and said that the man who is deceived by it is not a wise man.

For the Lord to say through Solomon in Prov. 23:29-35 that the wine that moveth itself aright, is fermented, produces woe, and sorrow, and contentions, and babbling, and wounds, and redness of eyes, and bites like a serpent, stings like an adder, causes men to go after strange women, utter perverse things, and produces insensibility to pain, and converts men into addicts, and says we are not to look upon that kind of wine, and then appoint that same demoralizing wine for use at the Holy Communion would be such an inconsistency and contradiction on His part that the harmony of the Scriptures would be upset and their divine inspiration would be refuted for God cannot contradict Himself. "I am the Lord, I change not" (Mal. 3:6).

If what the Lord appointed for us at the Lord's Supper to commemorate His incorruptible blood were fermented, then we have Him sanctioning what He previously condemned, and blessing what He previously forbade, and appointing what was corrupt as a symbol of Him whose body and blood did not "see corruption." It would be a contradiction indeed to use what was corrupt to symbolize the Holy One Who was not suffered to see corruption (Ps. 16:10; Acts 2:27).

Chapter 35

WHAT IS THE FRUIT OF THE VINE?

Whether Jesus used fermented or unfermented wine at the Last Supper must be determined by the meaning of the expression "the fruit of the vine," for it is definite that this is what was in the cup.

In the chapter "Tirosh — Unfermented Wine, The Fruit of the Vine," I quoted from McClintock and Strong's Cyclopedia of Biblical, Theological and Ecclesiastical Literature, Hitt, Douglas, Burns, Faussett, and gave Bible references which show that the Hebrew tirosh was vintage fruit, the produce of the vine, the fruit of the vine.

G.W. Samson made an extensive study on "Communion Wine," and inasmuch as the Cyclopedia of Temperance and Prohibition (1891) is no longer in print I give his article below.

"Communion wine. — The importance of the inquiry whether Jesus appointed intoxicating or unfermented wine for the communion service has interested in every age of the Christian Church able leaders who have regarded it a test of morality. While all the leading writers of the first five Christian centuries recognized that the wines made, drank and used at the Passover and Last Supper by Christ were the fresh 'fruit' of the wine, the difficulty of obtaining such wines in Africa and Northern Europe led no less than twenty fathers of the first five centuries, and, later, men like Photius of the Greek Church in the 9th Century, Aquinas of the Roman Church in the 13th Century, and Bingham of the English Church early in the 18th Century to an exhaustive study of methods of preparing unintoxicating wines, and to review the discussions and decisions of successive Christian Councils on communion wine as all-important in Christian morals. Its growing moral bearings, recognized in all branches of the Christian Church, has led on to the exhaustive research which now permits demonstrative conclusions. As the prior question whether Nazarites were to be excluded from the Passover or to be required to violate their pledge of abstinence is settled by the connected records of Numbers, 6th to 18th chapter, so Luke's connection, as a Greek physician acquainted with wines, or John's abstinence (1:15), of popular comment on it (7:33,34) and the 'fruit of the vine' used at both the Passover and communion observance (22:18, comp. Matt. 26:29, and Mark 14:25), is a necessary guide to an exhaustive and therefore conclusive decision as to the wine appointed for the Lord's Supper. With this prior consideration in view, the successive steps in research are the following: (1) Christ as a 'conforming Jew' must, as to the wine of the Passover, have strictly followed the Mosaic statute and the historic precedent which from the days of Moses to the present time has ruled the character of wine used in Hebrew rites. (See Passover Wine). (2) The word 'wine' is not used in the account of the Supper given by three evangelists; but the term 'fruit of the vine' is applied by Luke to the cup of the Passover (22:18), and by Matthew (26:29), and Mark (14:25) to the same cup used at Communion. (3) At no age, in no land and among no people, as among the Romans under their Republic, especially for two centuries before Christ, was the method of preserving wines free from intoxicating ferment so studied and practiced; while no class of men were so true to moral virtue as were the Roman Centurians mentioned in the lives of Christ and his Apostles; a fact noted by Matthew as a reproof to his countrymen (8:10; 27:54), and especially repeated by Luke, who wrote for cultured Greeks (7:2, 4, 5, 9; 23:47; Acts 10:1, 2, 7, 34, 35; 21:32; 22:25, 26; 23:27; 27:1, 3, 43; 28:16). (4) The fact that from the time of his making 'fresh wine,' Greek 'kalon' (John 2:10) for a wedding, to his rejection of wine on the cross, Jesus drank only unintoxicating fresh product of the grape, confirms not only the former facts stated, but the added fact that wine of Christ's Supper was the fresh product of the grape. (5) The allusions of Paul, the first to give a written account of the Lord's Supper (1 Cor. 12:20-26), have by the ablest Christian scholars from the 2nd to the 19th Centuries, been declared to have been conformed to Christ's example, for these reasons: First, Corinth furnished then, and the Greek Isles now export, preserved unfermented wine; Second, The term 'wine' is not used by Paul, as it was not by Christ; Third, The beverage in 'the cup' is supposed to be familiar. The Greek verb 'methuo,' found seven times (Matt. 24:49; John 2:10; Acts 2:15; 1 Cor. 11:21; 1 Thess. 5:7; Rev. 17:2, 6), means 'surfeit', not drunken, as does the noun 'methusma' in the Greek translation of Hos. 4:11; the contrast in 1 Cor. 11:21 being with 'hungry,' clearly relating to food, not to articles of drink.

"The facts as to the New Testament record relating to 'communion wine' are confirmed in each age succeeding the day of Christ and his Apostles. Clement in Egypt in the 2d Century alludes to the Christian 'Enkratites' or total abstainers; who, living in lower Egypt, had no vines; and who, citing the fact that in 1 Cor. 11 Paul does not mention wine but only 'the cup,' used water at the Lord's Supper. He mentions Greek sects as the Pythagorians, who drank no wine, but cites David's pure beverages, the fresh product of the grape; he declares that the cup of the Lord's Supper is the 'blood of the grape-cluster,' and, stating that the wine Christ made at the wedding was the same, he repeats Christ's words thus: 'This is my blood, the blood of the vine,' as alluding to John 15:1, in the figure 'I am the vine, and ye are the branches.' Origen in the opening of the 3d Century, alludes to three kinds of wine: the ordinary intoxicating wine, the wine diluted with water, and the 'sweet nectar' of Homer and of the Greeks, which he declares is Christ's appointment. Cyprian, at Carthage in Northern Africa, in the middle of the 3d Century, cites Melchisedec, quoted by Christ and Paul as well as David (Psa. 110:1,4; Matt. 22:44; Heb. 5:6; 6:20; 7:17,21) as prefiguring his sacrifice, and so his memorial Supper (Gen. 14:18); and, quoting Gen. 49:11, he asks, 'When here the blood of the grape is mentioned, what else than the wine of the cup of the Lord's blood is set forth?' He cites David's beverage of fresh grape juice in his shepherd life (Psa. 23:5), and the wine made fresh and declared 'the best' (optimum in Latin) as that used at the Supper. Zeno, at Verona in Northern Italy, in the 3d Century, states that the cup of the Lord's Supper was fresh 'grape juice' (mustum); he declares that it was the simple beverage of Melchidesec, Abraham, Joseph and Jesus in Palestine, and also like the Grecian 'gleukos' referred to Acts 2:13. Chrysostom, court-preacher at Constantinople at the close of the 4th Century, condemning the custom of wine-drinking, meets the objection that it was appointed for the Lord's Supper; and declares that Christ, foreseeing this perversion was careful in selecting the terms, 'I will drink no more of the fruit of this, the vine.' Jerome, who spent 30 years in Palestine at the close of the 4th and the opening of the 5th Century, that he might see, in the land where Jesus lived, and verify every fact of history, says of the wine of the Supper, citing Christ's words 'The fruit of the vine,' that it was fresh from the noble vine (Gen. 49:11), and like the 'tirosh' of Hos. 2:8, 9, 22. Augustine, going from Rome as a gospel herald to Carthage in the 5th Century, meeting the difficulty of providing fresh wine for the Lord's Supper and the perversion made of Christ's appointment, alludes to Virgil's mention in his Georgics of the simple country provisions of 'milk, honey and must.' He cites 'tirosh' blessed by Isaac, as Christ's beverage; and he declares that the cup of the Lord's table is what a little child may drink.

"In successive ages since these early Christian leaders saw how vital the question whether Jesus was behind the Greek and Roman patriots of his day in guarding his followers from perversion of his example and appointment, profound and conscientious scholars in every branch of the Christian Church, in lands where the vine and its richest fruits were not, as in Palestine, native to the clime, have previewed all this testimony. Thus, Photius, a leader in the separation between the Greek and Roman Churches in the middle of the 9th Century, in maintaining the custom of the Eastern Church, which administers the cup even to children, comments as a native Greek on Christ's words as to 'new wine' and 'the fruit of the vine' as taught in all former and subsequent ages. Aquinas, born in Italy but spending his early life in France and Western Germany, is called to remonstrate against the wine sometimes used; and retraces at great length the Old and New Testament history, showing that Christ used in his Supper fresh 'Wine of the vine;' urging that 'True wine can be carried to those countries where there are no vines, as much as is sufficient for the sacrament,' and stating that where grapes of inferior quality grow, as on the Rhine, 'This sacrament can be observed with must,' since 'must has already the character of wine.'

"In the difference that arose between the Protestant Episcopal Church and the various dissenting churches in the close of the 17th and the opening of the 18th Centuries, a thorough and exhaustive review of former authorities was made by Poole, as a scholarly and uncontroversial dissenter, and Bingham of the Established Church of England; both reaching like conclusions. The earnest spirit of Whitefield and Wesley reviewed a little later call for a return to a pure, unintoxicating wine for the Lord's Supper; and in the early part of the 19th Century Adam Clarke wrought conclusions of former scholars into his commentary. At the era of its publication, many conscientious Christian leaders, who from the era of Whitefield's first visit had longed and labored in New England for a return to Christ's pure appointment, found in Moses Stuart an intelligent advocate, though his declining age forbade exhaustive research. In 1829 John N. Barbour of Boston imported from the Grecian Isles, in bottle, pure wines, which when analyzed by the eminent Dr. John A. Warren were found free from alcohol. The progress of the popular demand by reformed inebriates, like Gough, and by students like Lees of England and Nott and others in the United States, has steadily confirmed the truth taught by Christ, and has promoted the 'grave' which his example and his appointment have inspired. The special confirmation which the monuments of Egypt have given as to the early methods of preparing and preserving unfermented wine, and the reopening of Palestine for the repetition of the studies of Jerome, and yet more, the revival in Italy and Spain, as well as in California, of ancient methods, has facilitated the return to the use of unfermented wine at the Lord's Supper specially sought in Great Britain and America by reformed inebriates."

To the above article by Samson, we add the following comments by Dawson Burns, whose book The Bases of the Temperance Reform (1873) is also no longer in print.

"1. It is said 'that by using wine in the ordinance of the Lord's Supper, the Saviour gave it a special honor inconsistent with the character ascribed to it by advocates of total abstinence.' Several points of consequence are overlooked by persons who raise this objection:

"(1) That the word 'wine' does not occur in the New Testament in reference to the institution and celebration of the Lord's Supper. The phrase used by the Saviour is 'the fruit of the vine,' and the apostle Paul simply speaks of 'the cup.' Those, therefore, who assume, contrary to evidence, that the Greek oinos always meant the intoxicating juice of the grape, gain nothing by the assumption, unless they show that 'the fruit of the vine' is also of necessity an inebriating fluid. Who, however, can pretend to advocate a proposition so utterly ridiculous? Who does not know that 'the fruit of the vine,' as it exists in its natural state, is not and never can be of an intoxicating quality; and that, when the expressed juice becomes so by passing through the fermenting process, it so far ceases to be the fruit of the vine and natural growth, and becomes the fruit of the vat? The wine of commerce can only claim to be considered the fruit of the vine to the extent that it is physically identical with the substance which the vine produces, and this identity can never be so complete as when the expressed juice of the grape is preserved and presented, in the sacramental service, chemically the same as it exists within the uncrushed cluster. Besides, it is notorious that, beyond the change in the grape-juice effected by fermentation, the adulterations of various liquors are so ingenious that the ablest connoiseurs cannot tell fabricated from genuine wine; and are so extensive that very few who purchase even the high-priced sorts can have any real guarantee of their genuine character; hence it is evident (1) that the unfermented juice of the grape is more really the 'fruit of the vine' than any fermented wine, however genuine; and (2) that the assurance of using the 'fruit of the vine' at all must be exceedingly slender in the great majority of cases where the wines of commerce enter into the sacramental service. It is also forgotten—

"(2) That as all ferment and fermented things were forbidden to the Jews at the Passover, when the Lord's Supper was instituted, it is more in accordance with the symbolical meaning of that prohibition (one which the apostle applies to Christians — 1 Cor. v. 6-8) to take the unfermented than

118

the fermented juice of the grape. We need not enter into the controversy whether the Jews celebrated their Passover with fermented or unfermented, if with the former, they must have broken their law; and whenever they do so now, they break their law; and those who assume that the Lord used such wine must also assume that he broke the law he came to fulfil (as a Jew) to the letter. Modern science has demonstrated (what careful observation must always have shown) that the fermentation of grape-juice is similar to the fermentation of bread or beer; and, therefore, that whosoever spiritual symbolism is conveyed by the absence of fermentation must be expressed more clearly by unfermented than fermented wine. . .

"(3) That as the Lord's Supper is designed to bring before the communicant the redeeming work of Christ as typified by his broken body and shed blood, there ought to be as close an analogy as is possible between the physical elements and the spiritual facts. The Redeemer himself was 'pure, undefiled, and separate from sinners,' and his work was like himself, and designed to conform us to his glorious image. Bread is a fitting representative of what is life-giving, for it is the staff of bodily life (and leavened bread does not lose this essential representativeness); but alcoholic wine is in reality wine mixed with an element hostile to health, life, virtue, and Christian excellence — it is wine which by fermentation has become a 'mocker' and 'defrauder;' and as soon as this fact is understood, the symbol loses its symbolic beauty and fitness, and the communicant is compelled to think of what the physical element ought to be, and not what it really is. But what need is there for this incongruity to subsist, when 'the pure blood of the grape' can be procured, and a true correspondence between the visible substance and the invisible reality can be established? The silly charge that total abstainers reject wine and prefer water in the eucharist is one of the idle tales by which ignorance and malice is accustomed to defame a principle unassailable by reason. The head and font of all the offending is that many of the friends of temperance desire to use, and to see used, in the celebration of the Lord's Supper, an article which is unquestionably 'the fruit of the vine,' rather than a liquor that is, at best, the fruit of the vine partially perverted, and that may not contain a single drop of the juice of the grape. The reader must judge for himself whether this preference is contrary to the example and will of the Redeemer in the institution of the Holy Supper."

It is most unfortunate that the works of these two writers and their associates are no longer available.

While studying the above from Burns, my mind was directed to a folder in my files which contains a Memorandum of the Federal Alcohol Tax unit. This memorandum gives concrete proof of the adulterations of wine as mentioned by Burns. I obtained this from a man who was an agent of the Alcohol Tax Unit. He formerly had been a Prohibition Agent, but with the repeal of the 18th Amendment was assigned to the Alcohol Tax Unit. He came to our office in Chicago when I was a radio commentator for The Temperance League of Illinois and gave me his copy of the memorandum, a

119

portion of which I give below:

"ADVISORY MEMORANDUM OF THE ALCOHOL TAX UNIT

"District No. 1 March 15, 1948

"No. 252 Winemakers may be permitted to use urea in the manufacture of wine, provided the amount used is limited to two pounds to 1,000 gallons of juice or wine.

"(signed) Daniel J. Conerty

"District Supervisor"

Urea is defined by Webster's Collegiate Dictionary, Fifth Edition, as "n. [N.., fr. F. uree, fr. Gr. ouron urine.] Biochem. a very soluble crystaline, nitrogenous compound, $CO(NH_2)2$, the chief solid constituent of the urine of man and other mammals." I have been told that before synthetic urea was developed some winemakers kept stables of horses, processed their urine, taking out the urea for use in wine making.

How could wine that is 14 percent alcohol, and contains two pounds of urea, whether animal or synthetic, to every 1,000 gallons of juice truly be considered "the fruit of the vine," and properly symbolize the incorruptible blood of Him Who was "pure and undefiled," and Whose body was not permitted "to see corruption?"

In the chapter "Tirosh — Unfermented Wine, The Fruit of the Vine," I showed that the Hebrew word tirosh meant vintage fruit, produce of the vine, the fruit of the vine. In Chapter 22 I gave Josephus' account of the dream Joseph interpreted for the butler which tells of his squeezing the juice from three clusters of grapes into a cup which was given immediately to Pharaoh, and how Josephus called this fresh grape juice gleukos and the fruit of the vine. If Josephus called unfermented grape juice "the fruit of the vine," what reason have we for assuming that Jesus meant anything else by the same expression?

By no stretch of the imagination can fermented wine that has practically all of its original 14 to 30 percent sugar destroyed, and is corrupted by as much as fourteen percent alcohol, and further adulterated by urea and other additives we have not mentioned, be called tirosh which both Jewish and Christian authorities say is always unfermented. Neither can it be called gleukos which is always unfermented, nor the fruit of the vine. But tirosh and gleukos are both properly called the fruit of the vine.

The cup Jesus took contained the fruit of the vine, tirosh, gleukos, unfermented grape juice.

Chapter 36

STRONG DRINK

Using the words strong drink to translate the Hebrew shekar or the Greek sikera has no defense. Shekar is rendered strong drink 21 times and strong wine once by the King James translators, and sikera which appears only once in the New Testament is rendered strong drink, but not once is either word preceded by, followed, or used in any way with a Hebrew or Greek adjective or modifier meaning strong. The word was added by the translators who misunderstood the meaning of shekar and sikera.

English speaking people of our day understand the words strong drink to mean high percentage alcoholic beverages such as: whiskey, gin, brandy, rum, vodka and other distilled beverages which are 35 to 75 percent alcohol. Such drinks were unknown to Israel in the time of Moses when the word shekar is first used in Lev. 10:9 and Num. 6:3 forbidding the priests and Nazarites to use it, and in Deut. 14:26 where the Israelites are told to purchase and use it at one of their holy festivals. Distilled spirits were not known to the Israelites of the Exodus and the use of the word shekar at this time would indicate the meaning of the word as it is used in later Scriptures.

Strong drinks are produced through distillation. Writers do not agree on the origin of alcoholic distillation. The Encyclopedia of Temperance and Prohibition says: "Intoxicating drinks have been used in China from the remotest times. The earliest historical records, which began at a period more than 2,000 years before the Christian Era, mention a spirituous liquor as an article already in common use and speak of the drunkenness of some of the early emperors and their ministers as a matter of shame and a source of calamity. The art of distillation, in all probability was first discovered by the Chinese, but at such an early date that there is no record of it. One tradition ascribes its invention to Tu K'ang, who Dr. Williams says was a woman of the Scythian Tribes. Dr. Legge however, says it is not known who Tu K'ang was. Another Chinese tradition declares that this liquor was first made by (Iti, probably) a cook in the household of Yu, who reigned in the 23rd Century before Christ. Dr. Edkins has denied that distillation was known among the Chinese before 1280 A.D., and would have us believe that this liquor was simply fermented. But Dr. Legge has shown that the phrase for distilled liquor, on which this argument turns, was used as early as 618 A.D. . . .

"There seems to be but little doubt that the ancient Chinese understood and practiced distillation many centuries before the Christian Era. . .The Chinese records relate that the discoverer (Iti) was disgraced, and that his name was held in loathing by subsequent generations. To the rest of the civilized world distillation was unknown until the art was gradually introduced from Arabia, where it was discovered in the 11th Century A.D. by Albucasis, a chemist."

Other temperance writers state that Albucasis of Arabia was the one who discovered alcoholic distillation, but this is not accepted by others who do not write from a temperance approach.

The World Book Encyclopedia is quite brief on the subject of distillation of alcohol saying: "Distilled Liquors are believed to have originated among the Chinese. The people of China made a strong drink from rice wine long before the Christian era. The Arabs carried the science of distilling to Europe in the Middle Ages. Brandy and whiskey were the first European distilled liquors." (1952 Edition, Vol. 1, P. 204).

The American Peoples Encyclopedia says: "Distillation is an ancient process. Many of the principles involved were discovered long before chemistry was developed as an exact science. In the third century B.C., Aristotle evaporated salt water and condensed the steam. In the first century A.D., Dioscorides treated wool flocks with steam and obtained distillates by wringing out the wool." (1953 Edition, Vol. 7, P. 7-159). On page 7-164 is this statement: "History of the Distilled Beverage Industry, The technique of distilling was known long before the Christian era by the Chinese, who made a spirituous liquor from rice wine. Arrack made from fermented palm juice, rice, and molasses is the oldest distilled beverage, having originated in the East Indies during the ninth century B.C. The Celts of ancient Ireland and Scotland produced the earliest form of whiskey from malted barley; the Russians discovered that vodka could be made from the fermented mash of wheat . . ."

To the above statements on the antiquity of distilled alcoholic beverages both Americana and Britannica Encyclopedias disagree and give a much more recent date for the discovery of alcoholic distillery.

Encyclopedia Americana says, "Although inebriating drinks were known centuries before, and were described in the ancient papyri, the Old Testament, and in manuscripts, it is fairly certain that these drinks were only the products of fermentation. The exact discovery of alcoholic distillation is uncertain, but may be ascribed with a good deal of justification to Salernus, a physician who lived in Salerno about the middle of the 12th century, and referred to it in his writings" (1957 Edition, Vol. 9, P. 173). "Whiskey was an early Gaelic invention — uisgebeatha, 'water of life' —made from grain instead of from grapes or other fruits. When the English invaded Ireland in 1170, they found the Irish already adept at distilling this liquor; the Scots (who spell their whisky with an 'e') are known to have been making it as early as that if not earlier" (P. 177).

On the subject of whiskey, Encyclopedia Britannica says: "The term is derived from the Celtic uisquebeatha, afterward contracted to uisquebaugh meaning water of life. The distillation of alcoholic beverages from fermented liquors became general throughout the whole of Europe during the 16th and 17th centuries but, while in the southern grape-producing countries wine is the liquor which is subjected to distillation, various types of grain are used in the north" (Vol. 23, p. 569, 1958 Edition).

About alcohol Britannica says: "Despite the Arabic origin of the word, the separation of alcohol from wine apparently was not known to the Arabian chemists. According to Edmund O. von Lippman their distillation apparatus did not possess adequate means for cooling to permit condensation of low boiling liquids. This point may well be questioned, but Marcellin Berthelot and Lippman both note that the earliest known description of the concentration of alcohol by distillation of wine occurs in a Latin manuscript of the 12th century, Mappae Calvicula. Since the 10th century version of this manuscript contains no reference to this process, it is assumed that alcohol first was separated by distillation around the 11th century in the wine districts of Italy" (Col. 1, p. 542, 1958 Edition).

This latter statement from Britannica does not agree with one in the 1929 Edition which credits the Arabians with discovering the distillation of alcohol from wine: "Distillation appears to have been used by earliest experimentalists. Aristotle (384-322 B.C.) mentions that pure water is made by the evaporation of sea-water. Pliny the elder (A.D. 23-79) describes a primitive method of condensation in which oil obtained by heating rosin is collected on wool placed in the upper part of the still. The Alexandrians added a head or cover to the still and prepared oil of Turpentine by distilling pine resin. The Arabians improved the apparatus by cooling the tube leading from the head, or alembic, with water, and discovered a number of essential oils by distilling plants and plant juices, alcohols from wine, and distilled water. By its use, the alchemists were enabled to study hydrochloric, nitric, and sulphuric acids in a relatively pure state" (Vol. 7, p. 427).

Funk & Wagnalls Standard Reference Encyclopedia attributes the discovery of alcoholic distillation to Abul Kasim, an Arabian physician: "The earliest alcoholic beverages were products of simple fermentation which at most, yields about 12% alcohol. The first mention of distillation on record was made by Abul Kasim, an Arabian physician, in the 10th century. At first only wine was distilled, but soon afterward other fermented products were employed." (Vol. 8, p. 2785, 1960 Edition).

From the above, it is clear that there is no consensus among historians as to when the technique of alcoholic distillation was first developed. If it was discovered by either Albu Kasim of Arabia, or Salernus of Salerno, in the tenth, eleventh, or twelfth centuries A.D., it is certain that the ancient Israelites knew nothing about distilled beverages.

Aristotle does mention the distillation of pure water from sea water in the 4th century B.C., but no mention is made of distilled beverages made from fruit juices. His silence on this matter gives strong support to the theory that distilled liquors were not known to the Greeks of his time, and if they were not known to the Greeks of the 4th century B.C. what evidence have we that they were known to the Israelites of an earlier period?

But what about the distilled beverages of the ancient Chinese? We have already shown that some question the report of the Chinese having distilled liquors two thousand years or more before Christ. The American Peoples Encyclopedia says that Arrack made from fermented palm juice, rice, and molasses is the oldest distilled beverage, having originated in the East Indies during the ninth century B.C. and this would be too late to have any bearing on Mosaic legislation which was given seven centuries earlier, or on the admonitions in the book of Proverbs concerning yayin (wine) and shekar (erroneously rendered strong drink).

Assuming, however, that the Chinese did have distilled liquors two thousand years Before Christ, there is no evidence that these drinks were obtained from China by the Israelites or that the Chinese communicated the art of alcoholic distillation to ancient Israel.

According to Archbishop Ussher's dates given in our English Bibles, Abraham entered Canaan in the year 2056 B.C. and it is quite certain that he had no commerce with the Chinese. The same can be said of Isaac and Jacob. In the year 1491 B.C., the Israelites made the exodus from Egypt. For four hundred years before this they were in bondage to the Egyptians, and all this time they did not communicate with the Chinese. It is true that the Egyptians had intoxicating drinks, but these were the product of fermentation only.

Right after leaving Egypt, and while encamped at Mt. Sinai, those who took the vow of a Nazarite were forbidden to drink either yayin (wine) or shekar (palm wine) during the time of their separation (Num. 6:1-21), and priests were forbidden to drink yayin or shekar when they went into the tabernacle (Lev. 10:8-11). From the time of Abraham's entrance into Canaan until the encampment at Mt. Sinai (and long after), the descendants of Abraham had no commerce with China, and the Chinese technique of distillation remained unknown to the rest of the world. However, yayin (wine) and shekar (palm juice, erroneously rendered strong drink) were familiar to the Israelites and used in their diets. And when Moses used these words the people understood what they meant.

Now if the word shekar meant that which is derived from tapping the palm tree, whether in its fresh form, in the form of sugar, a thick syrup, or fermented, while Israel was in the wilderness, when the first legislation was given concerning it, then we are to understand the word shekar means the same in subsequent legislation.

We have dealt with every Hebrew and Greek word in the Scriptures dealing with our subject. While some of the words we have studied are generic and include the meaning of a fermented beverage, not one of them can be interpreted to mean a distilled alcoholic beverage. None of them were more than 14 or 15 percent alcohol. I have shown that using the words strong drink to translate shekar is an inexcusable error.

The Arabs, who were cousins to the Israelites, did not have distilled alcohol until the time of Albucasis in the 10th century A.D. If Israel, whose territory bordered that of the Arabs, had the knowledge of distillation and used distilled beverages in the time of Moses, 2500 years before the time of Albucasis, it is indeed strange that their next door neighbors did not learn how to distill liquors until two and a half milleniums later.

The only word in the Hebrew Scriptures that is rendered strong drink in our English versions is shekar, and this is not a legitimate translation as I have shown in the foregoing pages. The strongest drinks the Israelites had could not have been more than 14 or 15 and in exceptional instances 16 percent alcohol, for when the alcoholic content reaches that percentage the yeast germs are inhibited from producing any more alcohol and fermentation ceases. Wines stronger than 16 percent alcohol are wines that have had alcohol added to make them stronger, and these are called fortified wines. They range from 16 to 25 percent alcohol.

The Host's Handbook, published by National Distillers Products Corporation, 1940 Edition, says that natural and sparkling wines range in alcoholic content from 11 to 14 percent alcohol. The fortified wines are natural still wines to which has been added brandy distilled from the same type of wine, in the last stages of fermentation. All sherries and ports are fortified.

The Standard Bartender's Guide, p. 198, says: "The alcoholic content of table wine is 14% or less . . . There are many sorts of wine, but only four broad categories: Natural still wines, such as Claret and Sauternes, containing 14% alcohol or less; sparkling, such as Champagne, 14% or less; fortified, such as sherry, 16 to 23%, and aromatized, such as vermouth 15 1/2 to 20%."

Unless wine is fortified by the addition of brandy to increase its alcoholic content it is never more than 14 to 16 percent alcohol. Very seldom do natural fermented wines reach 16 percent.

Beverages that are 35 to 75 percent alcohol, such as brandy, whiskey, gin, rum, vodka, which we consider strong drinks are the products of distillation of what has already been fermented. Brandy is made by distilling fermented wine. Whiskey and vodka are made by distilling the fermented mash of different grains. Gin is distilled from the mash of grain which has the juniper berry added. Rum is distilled from molasses. Arrack is distilled from fermented palm wine. Without distillation these strong drinks cannot be made.

Beverages produced in wineries through fermentation alone are not more than 14 to 16 percent alcohol. Britannica, Vol. 23, p. 666, 1958 Edition, and Americanna, Vol. 11, p. 127, 1957 Edition confirm the above statements that fermentation ceases when the alcoholic content reaches 14 or 15 percent.

I am giving all this to show that the ancient Hebrews did not have strong drinks as we have today simply because the process of distillation was unknown to them, and was not known to the rest of the world with the possible exception of China, and if the Chinese did have the technique of distillation, it remained a Chinese secret, just as the art of making gun powder and other things remained a Chinese secret for centuries.

The strongest drinks that ancient Israel had were not more than 14 to 16 percent alcohol. They may have added spices and drugs to their wine at times to increase their toxic strength, but they did not have strong drinks of a high alcoholic content. And in Prov. 23:29-35, one hundred forty-two words of dire warning are issued against the use of these fermented wines.

Using the words strong drink to translate shekar and sikera is an unjustifiable error. Especially is this so in regard to Deut. 14:26, "And thou shalt bestow that money for whatsoever thy soul lusteth after, for oxen, or for sheep, or for wine (yayin), or for strong drink (shekar)."

This verse has been used as a justification for drinking whiskey, gin, rum, cocktails, highballs, and other beverages of high alcoholic content. This writer knows persons who were total abstainers but have been led into the use of such drinks by a well known radio preacher who justifies their use by the way translators have rendered shekar in this verse. I possess a letter written by a staff member of the Bible college this man founded and operates ridiculing my position on abstinence, and stating that we are commanded to drink such beverages, using Deut. 14:26 as his proof text.

Shekar in this verse cannot refer to whiskey, rum, brandy, gin, vodka or other distilled beverages simply because distillation was not known or practiced by the Israelites. I have shown in previous chapters that shekar should have been rendered palm sap, sugar, or cider.

There are some texts in which the obvious meaning is the fermented palm sap, and in most of these places warnings, rebukes, or prohibitions are attached to the word. That God would sanction indulgence in a habit forming, addiction producing, mind altering, poisonous drug, especially at the time of a religious gathering, for the purpose "that thou mayest learn to fear the Lord thy God always" (Deut. 14:21-29), to me is unthinkable. Indulgence in strong drink leads away from the fear of the Lord.

While a student at the Institute of Scientific Studies, at Loma Linda, California, this writer received the following definition of alcohol in a lecture by Dr. Andrew C. Ivy: "Alcohol, from a pharmacological and medical viewpoint, is an intoxicating, hypnotic, analgesic, anesthetic, poisonous, and potentially habit-forming, craving-producing or addiction-producing drug."

The Lord knew all about the mind-altering, poisonous, addiction-producing nature of this drug when He gave Moses the law at Mt. Sinai, and to me it is bordering on blasphemy to say He would instruct Moses to tell Israel to spend their money for, and use such drugs at a religious gathering set apart for the purpose of teaching them to fear the Lord their God.

"Wine is a mocker, strong drink (shekar) is raging: and whosoever is deceived thereby is not wise" (Prov. 20:1). "Look not thou upon the wine when it is red, when it giveth his colour in the cup, when it moveth itself aright" (Prov. 23:31). "Woe to him that giveth his neighbour drink, that puttest thy bottle (poison) to him, and makest him drunken also" (Hab. 2:15).

It would be a self contradiction on the part of God Himself to tell Israel to buy and use that which He pronounces as raging and a deceiver, and forbids elsewhere. It would not be a contradiction for Him to tell them to buy yayin in the form of grapes, raisins, syrup, or unfermented grape juice, and shekar in the form of unfermented palm sap, sweet cider, syrup or sugar.

Chapter 37

SHEKAR FOR THE DYING MAN

"Give strong drink (shekar) unto him that is ready to perish, and wine (yayin) unto those that be of heavy hearts. Let him drink, and forget his poverty, and remember his misery no more" (Prov. 31:6,7).

The use of shekar and yayin in this text by no means justifies the common regular use of intoxicants. It was a practice in ancient times to give a stupefying drink to a condemned prisoner before he was taken to his execution. It was considered a means of tempering justice with mercy. We have a modern hangover of this in giving a man his choice of the last meal before going to the electric chair.

Wine was also given to persons in mental states that required sedation. Ferrar Fenton's Translation reads: "Give drink to the ready to perish; And wine to the bitter in mind; — Let him drink and forget his distress, and remember his misery no more."

Anesthetics, sedatives, and drugs used by physicians today were not known in ancient times. A sufficient amount of alcohol would have a sedative or analgesic effect on one in need of such medication. But Jesus said: "They that be whole need not a physician" (Matt. 9:12). Similarly, they that be whole need no anesthetics, analgesics, mind-altering, addiction-producing drugs.

It should also be noted that modern drugs are so much more effective that the ancient practice of using alcohol as an anesthetic or sedative is seldom resorted to in modern medicine.

In 1917 Dr. Charles H. Mayo said: "Medicine has reached a period when alcohol is rarely employed as a drug, being replaced by other remedies" (Fletcher Dobbins, Amazing Story of Repeal).

Dr. Arthur Dean Bevan, professor at Rush Medical College and former President of the American Medical Association said: "Viewed from the standpoint of modern scientific medicine, alcohol belongs to the groups of narcotics which consist of alcohol, ether, chloroform, chloral and similar drugs, such as sulphonal and veronal. The general actions of all the members are very much the same. They produce a first stage of imperfect consciousness and confused ideas, followed later by a stage of excitement, and if the dose is large complete unconsciousness which may, if the dose is sufficiently large, terminate in death. . .At the Presbyterian Hospital in Chicago, where we take care of more than twelve thousand patients a year, we have not yet prescribed through the drug room of the hospital a single bottle of alcoholic liquor since the passage of the prohibition amendment, and this is not due to any regulation against the use of alcohol. Any one of the attending medical men has the privilege of using alcohol if he sees fit in

127

the handling of his cases. It is due to the fact that there is little or no logical or scientific reason for the internal administration of alcohol in the modern treatment of disease. On the other hand the external use of alcohol has increased very markedly" (Fletcher Dobbins, Amazing Story of Repeal).

In Solomon's time modern sedatives, analgesics, anesthetics were not known. They used what they had. Today's drugs are so far superior that what was used in Solomon's day has now been discarded in favor of modern medicines. The fact that the ancients used alcohol as a sedative for persons in need of such medication by no means justifies the use of alcohol as a common beverage today.

Chapter 38

TIMOTHY'S INFIRMITY AND STOMACH WINE

"Drink no longer water, but use a little wine for thy stomach's sake and thine often infirmities" (1 Tim. 5:23). So wrote Paul to Timothy who was having trouble with his stomach. This advice given to an afflicted man 1900 years ago has been used by persons, who have nothing wrong with their stomachs, to justify their regular indulgence in beer, wine, whiskey, gin, rum, brandy, vodka, cocktails, highballs, and alcoholic concoctions of every description and potency, except the special stomach wine that was used in Bible days for dyspepsia.

Several things need to be understood about this verse which will give the reader an entirely different understanding of why Paul wrote as he did.

1. Some Bible scholars have noted that this is a parenthetic statement which is not a part of the theme that Paul is dealing with in the verses immediately preceding and following. Moffatt does not have this verse in the text of his translation but puts it in a footnote at the bottom and says: "The words, 'Give up being a total abstainer; take a little wine for the sake of your stomach and your frequent attacks of illness,' which follow, are either a marginal gloss or misplaced." Montgomery's Centenary Translation says in a footnote: "Verse 23 is apparently a marginal gloss, and not a part of the original letter." The New Catholic Bible recognizes the parenthetic nature of the verse but says in a footnote: "This abrupt parenthesis is characteristic of St. Paul." Whether or not the verse was a part of the original epistle will make no difference in our understanding of its meaning. We accept it as a part of the original letter.

2. Timothy was an abstainer from the use of wine. This is brought out clearly by other translations. Goodspeed, "Stop drinking nothing but water." Charles B. Williams, "Stop drinking water only." Amplified New Testament, "Drink water no longer exclusively." Montgomery's Centenary Translation, "Do not continue to drink nothing but water." The Twentieth Century New Testament, "Do not continue to drink water only."

It is apparent that Timothy was a total abstainer. These are the very words used in Moffatt's Translation, "Give up being a total abstainer." The Fermentists have never explained why Timothy abstained from wine and drank nothing but water. Apparently his convictions entered into what he ate and drank.

3. Timothy was having trouble with his stomach.

4. Timothy's stomach trouble was caused by the water he was drinking.

5. Paul could have prayed for his healing, but if Timothy had been healed and then continued to drink what was the cause of his illness it would be only a short time until his infirmity would return. It seems that Timothy did

get delivered at times, but the ailment would return. This is indicated by "thine often infirmities." What Timothy needed was not divine healing, but to stop drinking the alkali water that was upsetting his stomach.

6. Paul understood the situation and gave Timothy a word of advice about the water he was drinking and how to make it suitable for his stomach.

Timothy was a native of the city of Lystra in Lycaonia. At the time of Paul's letter to him, Timothy was at Ephesus. Both cities were in Asia Minor. The water in that region was strongly alkali and was upsetting Timothy's stomach. Paul was giving him advice on how to get rid of his disorder. It was a practice in those days, and it is still practiced in Syria, Mesopotamia, and other parts of Asia Minor, that when this alkali water was taken, it was mixed with syrup or jam made by boiling grape juice until it became thick. The properties in the grape juice neutralized the harmful properties in the water making it suitable for drinking.

Ferrar Fenton, in his book "The Bible and Wine," says, "1 Tim. 5:23: 'No longer drink water alone, but use with a little wine for the stomach, because of your frequent infirmities.'

"This advice of the Apostle to his friend is the favorite field of battle of those who claim the habit of using intoxicating drinks to be commanded to Christians. But St. Paul could hardly have so contradicted himself in his prohibition of the habitual use of intoxicating wine to the ministers of the Church as he had done (see 3:8 above), and a few lines afterwards have ordered Timothy, who held an Apostolic position in it, to regularly drink such liquor? It is only gross ignorance of the customs of olden times, and of the idiomatic use of the Greek language that originated the absurd import thus put upon St. Paul's words. 'Stomach Wine,' or 'Wine for the stomach,' the old writers upon Greek medicine tell us, was Grape-juice, prepared as a thick, unfermented syrup, for use as a medicament for dyspeptic and weak persons, and there cannot be a doubt but that was the 'Wine for the stomach' the Apostle told his friend to 'use' a little of mixed with water, which it is evident that Timothy, like other pious Jews of that period, restricted himself to, and had drunk previously, so as to avoid breaking the Levitical command against priests drinking 'Wine or strong drink' during the course of their ministry.

"However, as the passage has been made, by mistranslation and perversion, a serious stumbling-block, I venture to give it as it is in the Greek:

"'No longer drink water alone, but use with a little wine for the stomach, because of your frequent infirmities.'

"The Apostle's use of the dative case, which must be rendered in English by the adverb 'with,' indicates that 'a little stomach wine' should, as a medicant be mixed or 'mingled' as in other parts it is translated, with water, as the syrup anciently prepared from grapes and other fruits was done for use as a tonic to the stomach in cases of dyspepsia. When this fact is known, the absurdity of teaching that this bit of advice is a sacred sanction for always drinking intoxicant wine, in the place of water as a beverage, will be seen. Missionaries to Pagan nations ought especially to avoid repeating the false rendering of the versions of this Epistle, which are unfortunately by irreflection put into their hands."

Schirmacher says, "'Stomach wine,' or 'wine for the stomach,' according to the writers of old Greek medicine, was a grape juice prepared as a thick, unfermented syrup for use as a food for dyspeptic and weak persons! Pliny, who lived in the apostolic age, wrote: 'The beverage is given to invalids to whom it is apprehended that WINE may prove injurious.'"

Ernest Gordon writes: "Another practice was to boil the juice till thickened, store in skin bottles and keep in cool cellars. In the Georgics (1:295) one gets a picture of this operation. 'his wife . . . on the fire boils down the sweet juice of must and skims with leaves the wave of bubbling cauldron.' Hepsema was boiled down to one third, defrutum to one half. Before boiling it was treated with resonous gums or with sulphate of lime (gypsum): after boiling it was put into new wineskins. This unfermented paste, or treacle, was then used dissolved in water. This is what is meant in Scripture by mingling, or mixing wine. No better medicine for Timothy's 'stomach and oft infirmities' could have been recommended by Paul than the juice of the grape. It is, in fact, a specific, grape sugar being the one substance in nature which passes into the circulation without requiring digestion. One substance? No, there is one other. Alcohol passes unaltered to every cell of the human body, breaking down the lipoid defenses and exhibiting lethal affinities especially for nerve tissue. So again we have the duel between the life-giving grape and death dealing alcohol. One thinks of Dr. Legrain's bon mot: 'Alcohol is the illegitimate son of sugar.'

"Pliny mentions adynaton (wine without strength) 'which is given to invalids.' It is noticeable that Paul does not advise Timothy to drink wine but to use a little, presumably as medicine. This makes 1 Timothy 5:23 a very frail Magna Charta for alcoholic 'Christian liberty.'"

The following humorous incident related by the late Dr. Harry Rimmer, scientist, archeologist and writer on Christian apologetics as well as one of America's outstanding evangelical ministers, clears away any doubts concerning the true meaning of 1 Tim. 5:23.

"Recently a man came into my study who was not in a friendly and receptive mood. From his attitude we had reason to believe that he had probably been hen-pecked into coming by a concerned and anxious wife. It was necessary to open the windows because the magnificent flavor of the visitor's breath. He had scarcely introduced himself by name, than he blurted out in a bellicose and challenging fashion, 'What's wrong with a man taking a friendly drink occasionally? Doesn't the Bible say, 'Drink a little wine for your stomach's sake,' and didn't Jesus turn water into wine?'

"I looked the man over closely for a half a minute and classified him fairly accurately. I said, 'Yes, your reference is concerning wine in the book of Timothy. It is a medical prescription that was written to Timothy because of his stomach trouble. Is your name Timothy?'

"In some surprise the man said, 'No, my name is Bill.'

"I said, 'Is wine your favorite beverage?'

"He answered, 'No, I prefer gin.'

131

Intrigued by the man's honesty I further inquired, "Do you have stomach trouble?"

"He said, 'No, my stomach is all right, why?'

"I picked up the Scriptures and handed them to him saying, 'Show me the place where it says, 'Drink wine for your stomach's sake.'

"The man pulled away from the Word as though it had been a poisonous reptile and said, 'I wouldn't know where to find the place, but I am sure it is there.' So I opened to the reference under consideraton and said, 'A man named Timothy had been drinking the alkaline water of Asia Minor until he had ruined his digestion. A man named Paul wrote to him and sent him a medical prescription that would have some beneficial effect upon his local condition. Now, will you tell me, in all common sense, what relationship there is between a medical prescription for a sick man named Timothy concerning wine, and the casual drinking of a man named Bill, who has no physical ailment whatsoever?

"The man was somewhat taken aback and said, 'Well anyway he did tell him to drink wine.'

"I said to him, 'If you did drink wine, would you mix it with water?'

"The man was honest enough to say, 'No. Why spoil it? It is weak enough as it is.'

"It is a notable fact that those who cry the loudest about Paul's advice to Timothy and similar passages in the Scriptures would be the first to object to having water in their wine. Yet, the fifth chapter of First Timothy, and the 23rd verse should literally be translated, 'Drink no longer water alone, but mixed with a little wine for thy stomach's sake and thy frequent sickness.' The simple fact behind this Scripture is that the water of Asia Minor, heavily impregnated with alkali, was ruining Timothy's digestion. The common wine of that country was highly acid, more closely resembling our modern cider vinegar, than our sweet wines. A little of this acid put into the alkaline water would correct the evil effects. It was thus literally a medical prescription.

"The background of this story is interesting. Much of the water that a traveler met in antiquity was extremely disagreeable. It was the custom therefore for a tourist to carry on his person a small jar or container of a fruit preparation that had been boiled with sugar until it was about the consistency of thick molasses. When under the necessity of drinking the unpalatable water, the traveler would take spoonful of this heavy syrup and stir it into the cup to give it a pleasant flavor. This heavy fruit juice syrup which was made by boiling fruit juice with one third of its weight in sugar was called 'wine.' It was no more intoxicating however, than the jams and jellies of our day."

The above article was carried in The National Voice, and also included in The Voice of Temperance Scrap Book Number II, by Sam Morris.

Not long before his death, I had a conversation with Dr. Rimmer about the incident. He remembered the man's visit to his study and further said that he had just recently returned from Mesopotamia and that they still practiced the mixing of grape jam with their water and stated that one of the grapes grown in that area was similar to our own Concord grape which we use for making jams and jellies.

Dr. Rimmer mentioned the adding of sugar to the grape juice as it was boiled in ancient Mesopotamia. However, in other areas they boiled down the juice without the addition of sugar.

This writer has a minister friend who was born in Iran and told how his mother used to make this jam which was used, mixed with water, or spread on bread.

It is difficult to conceive of the Holy Spirit moving Paul to advise the ailing Timothy, whose stomach had been upset by drinking nothing but alkaline water, to remedy his condition by using an intoxicant which would further irritate the lining of his stomach. In using fermented wine, Timothy would be taking into an already upset stomach a membrane irritant, dehydrant, and poison in the form of alcohol. Alcohol does not build or repair cell tissue; it destroys tissue. It is an irritant, a dehydrant, a poison to a normal stomach and certainly would not be helpful to one already upset. Patients with ulcers are specifically warned against the use of alcohol because of its harmful effects.

In taking a four ounce glass of wine that is 12 percent alcohol a person would receive the same amount of alcohol that would be in a 12 ounce bottle of 4 percent beer, or a one ounce shot of 50 percent whiskey — a half ounce, and the alcohol in the glass of wine would be just as irritant as the alcohol in a shot of whiskey. But there would be no alcohol to irritate Timothy's already sensitive stomach in unfermented wine or grape syrup mixed with water.

Stomach wine or wine for the stomach was not an intoxicant. It was a non-alcoholic grape syrup or jam which was taken mixed with water for stomach ailments, and Paul's recommendation to Timothy in no way justifies the common, regular indulgence in intoxicants.

Like Dr. Rimmer, we wonder how many who quote Paul's statement would be willing to weaken their wine with water.

Chapter 39

WAS PAUL A MODERATIONIST?

"Let your moderation be known unto all men. The Lord is at hand" (Phil. 4:5). Because of the use of the word moderation here we are told that Paul taught moderation in the use of intoxicants and not abstinence.

Neither moderation nor abstinence is taught in this verse. The matter of indulging or abstaining from fermented beverages is not the subject of this verse. The Greek word epieikes rendered moderation deals with the disposition or trait of one's character. Thayer's Greek-English Lexicon says the word means, "seemly, suitable, equitable, fair, mile, gentle."

Epieikes is used in other places in the New Testament where it is translated patient or gentle. 1 Tim. 3:3, "Not given to wine, no striker, not greedy of fifthy lucre; but patient (epieikes), not a brawler, not covetous." In the first clause, Timothy is told not to be given to wine, but when Paul wanted to tell him to be patient, the Apostle used the word epieikes, which in Phil. 4:% is rendered moderation. "To speak evil of no man, to be no brawlers, but gentle (epieikes), shewing all meekness unto all men" (Titus 3:2). "Servants, be subject to your masters with all fear; not only to the good and gentle (epieikes), but also to the froward" (1 Pet. 2:18). "But the wisdom that is from above is first pure, then peaceable, gentle (epieikes), and easy to be intreated, full of mercy and good fruits, without partiality, and without hypocrisy" (James 3:17).

Every translation I have consulted clearly shows that the moderate use of intoxicants was not the meaning of Paul's statement in Phil. 4:5.

English Revised Version, "Let your forbearance (epiekes) be known unto all men." The margin says "gentleness."

The Twentieth Century New Testament: "Let your forbearing spirit be plain to every one."

Centenary Translation by Montgomery, "Let your reasonableness be recognized by every one."

Lamsa's Translation, "Let your humility be known to all men."

Numeric English New Testament by Panin, "Let your gentleness be known to all men."

Amplified New Testament, "Let all men know and perceive and recognize your unselfishness — your considerateness, your forbearing spirit."

Living Letters, The Paraphrased Epistles by Kenneth N. Taylor, "Let everyone see that you are unselfish and gentle in all you do."

Emphatic Diaglott Interleniar Translation, "The gentleness of you let be known to all men." New Version, "Let your gentleness be known to All men."

135

Englishman's Greek New Testament, "Your gentleness let be known to all men."

The New Catholic Bible, Confraternity Edition, "Let your moderaton be known to all men." Footnote says, "Moderation, the Greek signifies forbearance, a willingness to waive one's rights."

The Emphasized Bible by Rotherham, "Let your considerateness be known unto all men."

Moffatt's Translation, "Let your forbearance be known to everyone."

Concordant Version, "Let your lenience be known to all men."

The Companion Bible, commenting on the word moderation, says, "Moderation=forbearance. Gr. epiekes: adj." The marginal note says that this is the only place where the word is translated moderation and gives references to 1 Tim. 3:3; Tit. 3:2; Jas. 3:17; and 1 Pet. 2:18 where the same Greek word is used but translated gentle.

Weymouth, "Let your forbearing spirit be known to every one."

Fenton, "Let your good conduct be known to all men."

Charles B. Williams, "Let your forbearing spirit be known to everybody."

J. B. Phillips, "Have a reputation for gentleness."

The New English Bible, "Let your magnanimity be manifest to all."

American Standard Version, "Let your forbearance be known to all men." Footnote says, "Or, gentleness. Compare 2 Cor. 10:1."

Revised Standard Version, "Let all men know your forbearance."

Young's Literal Translation, "Let your forbearance be known to all men."

From the above renderings it ought to be clear to anyone that Paul is not writing Timothy to use intoxicants moderately. He is writing about mildness of temperament, patience, forbearance.

Chapter 40

DOES THE BIBLE TEACH TEMPERANCE?

"And as he reasoned of righteousness, temperance, and judgement to come, Felix trembled" (Acts 24:25). "But the fruit of the Spirit is love, joy, peace, longsuffering, gentleness, goodness, faith, Meekness, temperance: against such there is no law" (Gal. 5:22,23). "And beside this, giving all diligence, add to your faith virtue; and to virtue knowledge; and to knowledge temperance; and to temperance patience; and to patience godliness" (2 Pet. 1:5,6). "And every man that striveth for the mastery is temperate in all things" (1 Cor. 9:25).

Temperance is required of all who would live a godly life. But what is temperance? Again we come to a matter of definition. In Acts 24:25; Gal. 5:22,23; 2 Pet. 1:6 the Greek word is egkrateia. In 1 Cor. 9:25, and Titus 1:8 and 2:2 the Greek word is egkrateuomai.

Thayer's Greek-English Lexicon defines egkrateia as: "self-control, Lat. continentia, temperantia, (the virtue of one who masters his desires and passions, especially his sensual appetites.)" Thayer's definition of egkrateuomai is: "to be self-controlled, continent; to exhibit self-government, conduct one's self temperately." Then the definition goes on to say in regard to 1 Cor. 9:25: "in a figure drawn from athletes, who in preparing themselves for the games abstain from unwholesome food, wine, and sexual indulgence." Notice the words "abstain from unwholesome food, wine."

The true meaning of temperance has been perverted so that to many it means indulgence in intoxicants but not to excess. This is not the original meaning of the term. Temperance is not indulgence at all in what the Bible condemns. Temperance is the proper use of those things which are beneficial and good, and total abstinence from those things which are harmful and bad, such as intoxicating beer, wine and liquor.

This is not a biased opinion of the writer. Zenophon, who lived 434 to 355 B.C. gave two definitions of temperance. One meaning was, "moderation in healthful indulgence," and the other meaning was, "abstinence from things dangerous, as the use of intoxicating wines."

The meaning of temperance in Bible times did not provide for indulgence in things which were dangerous or intoxicating. These were condemned.

Funk & Wagnalls Desk Standard Dictionary, 1946 Edition, defines temperance as: "1. The state or quality of being temperate; habitual moderation, especially in the indulgence of any appetite. 2. Specifically, the principle and practice of total abstinence from intoxicants."

Funk & Wagnalls Standard Family Dictionary, 1961 Edition, Vol. II, defines temperance: "noun 1 The state or quality of being temperate; habitual moderation, especially in the indulgence of any appetite. 2 Specifically, the principle and practice of total abstinence from intoxicants. 3 (obs.) Calmness; self-control.—adj. 1 Of or pertaining to public places where alcoholic beverages are not sold. 2 Of or pertaining to movements, organizations, periodicals, speeches, etc., promoting total abstinence from intoxicants."

According to these definitions, when speaking in generalities about temperance it means moderation in the indulgence of any appetite, but when speaking specifically about intoxicants temperance means total abstinence. A temperance organization is an organization that promotes total abstinence from intoxicants. An organization that promotes the moderate use of alcohol cannot be called a temperance organization. A temperance magazine is one that promotes total abstinence from intoxicating beer, wine or liquor. A magazine that promotes the moderate use of such beverages cannot be called a temperance magazine. A temperance speaker is one who promotes total abstinence. A speaker who advocates moderation in the indulgence of alcoholic drinks cannot be called a temperance speaker.

These definitions are in agreement with Zenophon's definition of temperance 400 years before Christ. They agree with the meaning of temperance in the time of Christ and His Apostles. And they are the meaning of temperance today. Yes, the Bible does teach temperance.

Chapter 41

DID JESUS CONVERT WATER INTO FERMENTED WINE?

John 2:1-11 tells of the first mircle performed by Jesus at the wedding in Cana of Galilee, when He turned the water into wine (oinos), "and manifested his glory" (v. 11).

One Wine Theorists have used this miracle of Cana to justify the use of alcoholic beverages. Wine, they say, of necessity must be fermented; otherwise it is not wine, but a mere fruit juice. I have pointed out numbers of times in this treatise that oinos was a generic word with multiple meanings, and unfermented grape juice is oinos as well as fermented grape juice.

Let us briefly review what took place at this wedding. Jesus, His mother and His disciples were guests at a marriage celebration in Cana of Galilee. During the feast they ran out of oinos. The mother of Jesus told her Son they had run out. There were six waterpots setting near by and Jesus told the servants to fill them with water, which they did. He then told the servants to take some out and bear it to the governor of the feast. When the governor tasted it, he said it was the best oinos that had yet been served. Then he told the bridegroom: "Every man at the beginning doth set forth good wine; and when men have well drunk, then that which is worse: but thou hast kept the good wine until now. This beginning of miracles did Jesus of Cana of Galilee, and manifested forth his glory; and his disciples believed on him."

In changing the water into oinos (wine), Jesus did in a few minutes what He does through nature in a process of months. Water provided by nature is taken up through the vine (Greek, oine) and transformed into grape juice (oinos) in a process of months. Jesus accomplished this transformation in a matter of minutes. If the Lord can turn water into oinos in a few months time, why should we consider it impossible for Him to do the same thing in a few minutes during an emergency?

But was this wine fermented or not? This is the question that must be answered.

The Scriptures make it clear that Jesus Christ is God "manifest in the flesh." Jesus of the New Testament is Jehovah of the Old. This being so, He is the author of the Old Testament. It is His divine Word.

In Hab. 2:15, He said, "Woe unto him that giveth his neighbour drink, that puttest thy bottle (khamah, poison) to him and makest him drunken." If the Lord Himself had made fermented wine, it would still contain alcohol which is a mind-altering, habit forming, addiction producing, poisonous drug. In Prov. 23:29-35 the Lord condemned fermented wine as a creator of woe, sorrow, contention, babbling, wounds without cause, redness of eyes. He states that it bites like a serpent and stings like an adder, makes men to behold strange women and utter perverse things, induces insensibility, produces addiction so that men seek it again after having experienced the wounds, sorrow and woe that are its by-products. Added to all these maldictions is His commandment, "Look not thou upon the wine when it is red, when it giveth his colour in the cup, when it moveth itself aright."

How can the Lord sanction in the New Testament what He condemned in the Old? Would not His providing fermented wine at the marriage in Cana be giving His neighbour drink and putting the khamah (poison) to him? Would not this be a violation of His own commandment? Can the Lord do in the second chapter of John what He condemned in the second chapter of Habakkuk?

The fact that He is Lord makes it impossible for Him to contradict Himself, violate His own commandment, or change His attitude toward evil. He said of Himself in Mal. 3:6, "I am the Lord, I change not." Heb. 13:8 says, "Jesus Christ the same yesterday, and to day, and for ever." He cannot change in His attitude toward evil, or that which produces evil. The Lord cannot do Himself in the New Testament what He condemned others for doing in the Old Testament.

We are told that proof that Jesus provided the guests with fermented wine is found in the words of the governor in verse 10: "Every man at the beginning doth set forth good wine; and when men have well drunk, then that which is worse," The expression "well drunk" indicating that the guests were intoxicated, and therefore the wine they had been drinking was fermented. So the wine Jesus made must have been fermented also.

I have already shown that the expression "well drunk" (Greek methusthosin) in John 2:10 does not mean intoxication here, but satisfaction, having taken sufficiently to gratify.

I rebel at the thought that the guests at this marriage were already in a state of intoxication and that the Lord "manifested His glory" (John 2:11) by miraculously furnishing them with six waterpots more of an intoxicant that could only increase the debauchery. How could the Lord "manifest His glory" by making it possible for such drunkenness to be prolonged or increased?

On the other hand, if they had been drinking unfermented wine, there would be no inconsistency in Jesus providing the feast with a nonintoxicant more delicious than what they had been enjoying. This certainly would "manifest His glory."

If as we are told the words "well drunk" indicate that they were inebriated, how would they be in a position to recognize that which was better inasmuch as their sense of taste would have been dulled and their minds stupefied?

He who said in Hab. 2:15, "Woe unto him that giveth his neighbour drink, that puttest thy bottle (khamah, poison) to him, and makest him drunken," cannot provide a drink, a poison, in John 2:10 which will make men drunk or increase their drunkenness.

Chapter 42

WERE METHODS OF PRESERVING WINE UNFERMENTED KNOWN IN BIBLE TIMES?

We are told that methods of preserving grape juice unfermented were not known in Bible times, therefore the wine used at the Last Supper had to be fermented inasmuch as Passover came in the spring and the juice from the grapes harvested in the preceding fall could not have lasted that long without fermenting. This is also given as the reason why the new wine that the mockers on the Day of Pentecost said the 120 had been drinking was fermented.

Of course, this is contrary to the facts of history. It was a common practice in Bible times to preserve the sweet grape juice in an unfermented state.

G.W. Samson writes: "At no age, in no land and among no people, as among the Romans under their Republic, especially for two centuries before Christ, was the method of preserving wines free from intoxicating ferment so studied and practiced."

Samson further writes about the ancient Egyptians preserving unfermented wine: "This was prepared, as representations to the life on Egyptian tombwalls indicate, by drawing off from the top of the vat through a strainer, or in a twisted sack, the sweet watery juice of the grapes, dipping it at once into oiled jars, and covering it with a film of olive oil — a method now revived and employed by New York importers from Italy and Spain. This method was tested in February, 1881, at the Columbia College School of Mines, New York, when strained grape-juice put up in a glass phial covered with olive oil in October 1879, was found not to have the least trace of alcoholic fermentation."

If grape juice could be preserved by this method in the year 1879 A.D., why would it not work in Bible times? Samson tells us that it did work and the ancient Egyptians used this method. The Israelites had close intercourse with the Egyptians, having been in Egypt for four hundred years, and then carrying on commerce with them after entering Canaan. Why then should we believe that Israel was not familiar with this method of preservation?

The use of olive oil, however, was not the only method of preserving grape juice unfermented.

Ferrar Fenton in his book The Bible and Wine, referring to Valerius Masimus, Book ii. 1, 5; vi. 3; Aulus Gellius, Box x. 23; Pliny xiv. 13, writes: "Fermented wine was rare in early Roman times; — was only used as an act of worship in the Temples, and men under thirty years of age, and women all their lives, were forbidden to use it, except at the Sacrifices. Fresh grape-juice was called Mustum, and to make it keep without fermentation it was boiled until it became thick, like our treacle, or molasses, and in that state was named defrutum, that is, 'made from fruit,' and stored away in large jars for future use, to be eaten spread upon bread, as we do butter or treacle, or mixed and stirred up in water, as we do sugar in tea, to make a drink, as stated above. The Greek scientist, Aristotle, says that by keeping for a time in the skins or jars, it became as thick as butter, and had to be cut out by spoons. The Roman writer, Pliny, records that when the Grape-juice was boiled to one-third of its bulk, to secure the finest flavor, — that is, to be made into the 'Best Wine,' — it was called Sapa, from which word comes our vocables, 'sapid,' well-flavored, and 'savory,' delicious in taste."

Fenton continues: "To give variety of flavor, herbs and spices were often boiled in the juice during its preparation. Such was the 'Best Wine' of the Ancients, the sweetest and nicest flavored to the taste, — not as we imagine and mean, the most intoxicating, when we speak of 'Best Wine.'"

Ernest Gordon, in a quotation from Dr. Abbott, speaks of this method of preservation: "Dr. Lyman Abbott was in his day no friend of the Antialcohol movement, yet he can be considered a reasonably competent scholar. In his 'Dictionary of Religious Knowledge' he says of wine (p. 973); 'Fermented wine was the least common (in Biblical days) and the percentage of alcohol was small. New wines were wholly without alcohol and were easily preserved in this condition for several months. There were also wines in which, by boiling or by drugs, the process of fermentation was prevented and alcohol excluded. These were mixed with water and constituted the most common drink of the land."

Gordon continues: "The great classical authority on agriculture, Columella, writes (Book 12, ch. 29): 'That your grape juice may be always as sweet as when it is new thus proceed. After you apply the press to the grapes, take the newest must, put it in a new container (amphora), bung it up, and cover it up very carefully with pitch lest any water should enter; then sink it in a cistern or pond of cold water and allow no part of the amphora to remain above the surface. After forty days take it out. It will remain sweet for a year."

Lucius Junius Moderatus Columella was a latin writer who was born in Spain but lived in Rome in the first century A.D. and was contemporary with Senecca. He wrote extensively on agriculture and trees. If this was a method of preserving unfermented wine in Columella's day, then wine preservation was practiced in the time of Christ and His Apostles.

Gordon also tells of another method of preservation, and includes a quotation from the Georgics. The Georgics, written by Virgil (Vergil), a Roman poet who was born on Oct. 15, 70 B.C. and died Sept. 21, 19 B.C., has a poetic treatise dealing with the tillage of the fields, the rearing of herds and flocks, breeding of horses, keeping of bees, and one of the four books treats of trees, and especially of the vine and olive, which were the two great staples of the national wealth and industry of Italy. The statement of Virgil (Publius Vergilius Maro) is important because it gives testimony to the fact that before the time of Christ methods of preserving grape juice unfermented were known and practiced.

Gordon says: "Another practice was to boil the juice till thickened, store in bottles and keep in cool cellars. In the Georgics (1:295) one gets a picture of this operation. 'His wife . . . on the fire boils down the sweet juice of must and skims with leaves the wave of bubbling cauldron.' Hepsema was boiled down to one third, defrutum to one half. Before boiling it was treated with resinous gums or with sulphate of lime (gypsum): after boiling it was put in new wineskins. This unfermented paste, or treacle, was when used dissolved in water. This is what is meant in Scripture by mingling, or mixing, wine."

Fenton tells us this grape syrup or jam was called sapa by the Romans. The Latin word is cognate with the Hebrew word sobe (also sobhe, sobeth, sove, soveh, soba, cobe). I have already shown that according to Burns, Samson, Hitt and Douglas the Hebrew sobe like the Latin sapa was made by boiling the juice until thickened into a syrup or jam. I have also shown that the Hebrew words yayin and tirosh, like the Greek oinos, included this jam or syrup as one of the several meanings of these words.

The stomach wine Paul advised Timothy to use was also this jam mixed with water.

In addition to the above methods of preserving grape juice, the ancients dried the grapes, and in addition to making raisin cakes, they would boil the raisins in water and use the raisin juice for wine.

While in Europe during World War II, I served with a chaplain who used boiled raisin juice for communion. The mess sergeant would boil the raisins and this unfermented raisin wine was used for the Lord's Supper in Divine Services on the field.

Methods of preserving unfermented grape juice were certainly known in Bible times. The argument that since the grape harvest was at least eight months before Pentecost and there were no known methods of preserving the juice without fermentation is proof that the new wine of Acts 2:13, and the fruit of the vine that Jesus and the twelve drank at the Last Supper was fermented is without support from the facts of history.

In regard to the 120 on the Day of Pentecost, they were neither full of fermented wine nor unfermented wine. "They were all filled with the Holy Ghost."

Chapter 43

WHEN IT MOVETH ITSELF ARIGHT

"Look not thou upon the wine . . . when it moveth itself aright" (Prov. 23:31). This is a description of fermentation. Fermentation is the process whereby sugar in the grape juice is changed into alcohol (C_2H_5OH) and carbon dioxide (CO_2). The amount of alcohol and carbon dioxide (carbonic acid gas) produced by fermentation depends upon the amount of sugar contained in the fresh grape juice.

Water and sugar are the chief constituents of grape juice, as much as 97 percent or more. The amount of each varies in different kinds of grapes, some varieties having more sugar than others. The water and sugar content is also governed by the weather, seasonal rainfall, and the kind of soil the grapes are grown in. A dry season will produce grapes with a water and sugar content different from a rainy season. The water content of grapes may vary from 55 to 85 percent, and the sugar content may vary from 12 to 30 percent, and in some seasons even more.

During fermentation, the yeast germs convert the sugar into almost equal amounts of alcohol and carbon dioxide. Pasteur found that 100 grams of sugar in the juice would produce approximately 48.4 grams of alcohol and 46.6 grams of carbon dioxide. It is a rule of thumb that if you know the percentage of sugar in the grape juice, by dividing that figure by two, you can estimate fairly accurately the percentage of alcohol that will be present in the fermented wine.

Grape juice that is 20 percent sugar will have an alcohol content of about 10 percent when fermented, two parts of sugar making one part of alcohol. This is not an absolute rule for grape juice with higher amounts of sugar than 30 percent will not produce wine that is higher than 14 or 15 percent alcohol. When the alcohol reaches that high percentage it has an intoxicating effect on the yeast germs and they are inhibited from producing any more. The fermentation ceases. Some exceptionally strong yeast germs have been known to ferment wine that is as much as 16 percent alcohol, but this rarely happens.

"When it moveth itself aright." This action develops in the vat during the process of fermentation in which carbon dioxide is produced and is trying to escape. The bubbles that the housewife sees rising to the top of a spoiled jar of fruit are bubbles of carbon dioxide. When the pressed juice is put into the vat, in a few days it begins to move itself. The must begins to heave and solid matter begins to rise to the top forming the hat, or what the French call the chapeau. If a hole is made in the hat, the juice beneath bubbles and foams up through it. The bubbling makes a gurgling sound similar to the hum of swarming bees. This bubbling action becomes more violent as the fermentation developes, and the sound becomes louder. The carbon dioxide is rising to the surface of the vat where it escapes into the room.

In fermenting cellars, forced draft ventilation is now provided in modern wineries because of the danger of inhaling the poisonous carbon dioxide fumes. In wineries where ventilation is not provided strict rules against entering or approaching the vats during violent fermentation are enforced. Persons have been suffocated to death by the gas which is heavier than air and gradually displaces it from the floor up. Workers entering poorly ventilated vat rooms during fermentation usually take lighted candles with them. If the carbon dioxide is too thick for safety, the candles will go out and the worker is warned of the danger.

During fermentation, the solids in the vat continue to rise to the surface and this hat must be broken up, usually two times a day, for the best results in the finished wine. Wagner states that in Burgundy the wine makers used to break up the hat (chapeau) by taking off their clothes and getting into the vat naked, and thrashing about until they were exhausted or could no longer stand the fumes.

This may seem revolting and unsanitary to the reader, and it is both, but actually a naked man thrashing about in a winevat breaking up the hat could not produce as much harm as the alcohol contained in wine produced in the most sanitary condition.

What has been described here in the bubbling, gurgling, heaving, surging that takes place in the winevat is what the Lord meant when He said, "Look not thou upon the wine . . . when it moveth itself aright." Why this admonition? Because of what this kind of wine does to the man who drinks it. When this wine is completely fermented, the yeast germs have produced all the carbon dioxide and alcohol they are able to produce, "at the end it biteth like a serpent and stingeth like an adder." It produces woe, sorrow, redness of eyes. It causes men to forget their marriage vows and look upon strange women, and utter perverse things. It produces insensibility, and alcohol addiction. Because of the end result of this produce of fermentation, the Good Lord in love and wisdom admonishes us not to look up it (Prov. 23:29-35). "Look not thou upon fermented wine."

The fruit of the vine does not produce such end results. The fruit of the vine may be as much as 30 percent sugar, but it contains no alcohol. Fermented wine has practically all the sugar destroyed, and may be as much as 14 percent alcohol, and it may have other additives in it that are not in the fruit of the vine.

"Look not thou upon the wine . . . when it moveth itself aright."

Chapter 44

NOT GIVEN TO MUCH WINE

1 Tim. 3:2,3,8,11, "A bishop must be blameless, the husband of one wife, vigilant, sober, of good behaviour, given to hospitality, apt to teach; Not given to wine, no striker, not greedy of filthy lucre; but patient, not a brawler, not covetous . . . Likewise must the deacons be grave, not double-tongued, not given to much wine, not greedy of filthy lucre . . . Even so must their wives be grave, not slanderers, sober, faithful in all things."

Titus 1:7, "For a bishop must be blameless, as the steward of God; not selfwilled, not soon angry, not given to wine, no striker, not given to filthy lucre."

Titus 2:2,3, "That the aged men be sober (margin — vigilant), grave temperate, sound in faith, in charity, in patience. The aged women likewise, that they be in behaviour as becometh holiness, not false accusers, not given to much wine, teachers of good things."

In the two expressions, "not given to wine, not given to much wine," The moderationists say that we have an implied sanction or consent to drink wine in moderation, and only the taking of "much wine" is what the Apostle forbids in these two terms.

Taking the implied consent interpretation here gets the moderationists into immediate difficulty. We are taught that one way to prove the fallacy of an argument is to assume it to be true, then follow it to its logical conclusion where its falsity is exposed. We shall examine these verses by using this method and see what the results are.

We shall assume that "not given to much wine" gives implied consent to drinking wine in moderation. The restriction in Titus 2:3 is "not given to much wine." But to whom is this restriction applied in this verse? "The aged women!" Nothing is said about younger women. If the prohibition is limited to much wine," then the prohibition is also limited to "the aged women," for they are the only ones to whom Paul applies this restriction in his Epistle to Titus. The younger women are not mentioned by Paul, and being thus omitted would they not have an implied consent to "be given to much wine?"

Similarly, the restriction in 1 Tim. 3:8, "Likewise must the deacons be grave, not doubletongued, not given to much wine," inasmuch as it is addressed to the deacons, can be interpreted to give implied consent to those who are not deacons to be "doubletongued" and "given to much wine."

In 1 Peter 4:3,4 we have another problem that the implied consent position presents, "For the time past of our life may suffice us to have wrought the will of the Gentiles, when we walked in lasciviousness, lusts, excess of wine,

147

revellings, banquetings, and abominable idolatries: Wherein they think it strange that ye run not with them to the same excess of riot speaking evil of you." "Excess of riot." If only "excess of wine" is evil and we have an implied consent to wine in moderation, by the same token "excess of riot" can be construed to give implied consent to riot in moderation.

The phrase "not given to wine" is addressed to bishops. Would the implied consent advocates have us to understand this gives implied consent to those who are not bishops to be "given to wine?"

We must beware of construing any Scripture to mean or imply what was not intended by the writer, for "holy men of God spake as they were moved by the Holy Ghost" (2 Peter 1:21), but this is what the implied consent position does.

It is clear that more study must be given to these expressions. It is the position of this writer that there is no implied sanction or consent at all in these words of the Apostle and a study of the true meaning of the Greek words that are thus translated, and reference to other Scriptures will show this to be so.

Two rules of Bible hermeneutics are violated by the implied consent interpretation. Proper Biblical interpretation (hermeneutics) does not build a doctrine on an isolated passage of Scripture which seems to teach or imply one thing when the preponderance of the other Scriptures conform to the one isolated passage, but rather seek to harmonize that passage with the teaching of the rest of the Scriptures. The implied consent interpretation ignores this rule, as we shall see.

Another rule of Biblical interpretation is: when seeking to understand certain expressions in the Bible, we must keep in mind that we are dealing with writings that are two thousand to three thousand five hundred years old. They are expressions of an Oriental people who spoke different languages than we speak, and used terms peculiar to their customs which they clearly understood, but which we may not use or understand today.

The languages used by these people were Hebrew, Chaldean, and Greek. In these languages they had idiomatic expressions which at times meant things entirely different in their day from what these expressions mean to us in the English language two thousand or more years later. An idiom is an expression peculiar to a language not readily understandable from its grammatical construction or from the meaning of its component parts, as "to put up with" (meaning to tolerate, endure), the language or dialect of a region or people, the special terminology or mode of expression of a class, occupational group, etc. To illustrate, I gave one of my books to a lady in Alabama to give to her pastor. She told me, "He was sho proud to get it." We in north would say, "He was glad to get it."

"Not given to wine," is a poor translation of a Greek idiom, and a very poor translation as we shall see. The Greek is "me paroinon." Like a row of standing dominoes falling when the first is knocked down, translators have fallen by taking their cues from preceding translators who did not give proper study to the Greek text, the customs, and idiomatic expressions of the day when these Epistles were written.

148

No Greek word meaning to give or be given to is found or even implied in these two words. "Me" is a negative word meaning not. "Paroinon" is the combination of two words — para and oinon. Thayer says para is a preposition denoting proximity — at, by, near, by the side of, beside. Oinon of course is wine. Paroinon means near wine. That near, beside, by is the meaning of para is shown in our English word parable, which derives from the Greek parabolo which Thayer says means, "to put one thing by the side of another for the sake of comparison, to compare, liken." Me paroinon means not near, not beside, not close to wine. Young defines paroinos, "one along side of wine."

William Patton writes, "'Not given to wine' is certainly a very liberal translation, and shows how the usages of the day unconsciously influenced the translators. 'The ancient paroinos was a man accustomed to attend drinking parties.' Thus the Christian minister is required not only to be personally sober, but also to withhold his presence and sanction from those assemblies where alcoholic drinks are used, endangering the sobriety of himself and others."

Lees writes, "So Paul deemed a special and extreme form of abstinence proper to be urged upon a bishop; just as the Law Book of the Ante-Nicene Church commands that a bishop shall not enter a tavern, except on necessity."

Before saying that a bishop must be me paroinon, not be near wine, Paul uses another word in the same sentence which requires a bishop to abstain from the use of wine.

"A bishop then must be blameless, the husband of one wife, vigilant." The Greek word for vigilant is nephaleon. Implied consent advocates have overlooked this word. Strong shows that nephaleos derives from nepho which he says means to abstain from wine.

Patton writes, "Vigilant. — The Greek is neephalion, which Donnegan's Lexicon renders 'abstemious, that abstains, especially from wine' . . . In the adjective form, the word occurs only in 1 Tim. 3:2,11, and Tit. 2:2, from the word nepho, which Donnegan defines, 'To live abstemiously, to abstain from wine.'"

Lees comments are important here, "NEEPHO is found in the apostolic exhortations seven times; in its adjective form (neephalios) thrice. It occurs in such peculiar connections, that it seems absurd to put upon it any secondary or metaphorical meaning. The primary sense of the word, beyond all cavil, is that of ABSTINENCE; its secondary sense of 'wakeful' expresses the condition in which people who abstain from narcotics. 'Without doubt,' says Dean Alford, 'the word signifies abstinence; but Dr. Lees is bound to prove that it means total abstinence!' Now he is bound to prove no more than this, — that it means not drinking, and that the apostles use it, or ever may have used it, in that, its primary and proper sense. Josephus, one of their contemporaries, says of the priests, 'They abstained from wine' — (apo akratou neephontes). Does this admit doubt? Besides, Paul and Peter use the word along with the proper words for mental temperance and for watchfulness. Thus: —

"1 Thes. v. 6. Let us watch and drink not (neephomen).

"1 Pet. iv. 7. Be sound-minded and ABSTINENT unto prayer.

"1 Pet. v. 8. (Neepsate) Drink not, be vigilant . . . because your advarsary seeketh whom he may drink down [kata-piel]. (So Dr. A. Clarke, the commentator.)

"To enquire why Josephus, Philo, and others should by this word mean 'abstinence from drink,' while the apostles signify 'drinking a little' would be to follow perversity and appetite unto the den of lions.

"Josephus says of the Jewish priests, that, 'on account of their office, they had prescribed to them a double degree of purity.' So Paul deemed a special and extreme form of abstinence proper to be urged upon a bishop: just as the Law Book of the Ante-Nicene Church commands that a bishop shall not enter a tavern, except on necessity.

"St. Paul uses a word which is equivalent to the modern pledge, — 'discountenance the drinking usage,' — namely, nee (not) — par (over, or in presence of) — oinon (wine). In 1 Tim. iii. 2, 3, and Titus i. 7, 8, in connection with being no drinker, sound-minded, and no striker, it is commanded that a bishop shall be nee-par-oinos, 'not near wine,' not in its company. (So Professor Stuart.)"

Burns writes, "They enforced the virtue of sobriety—freedom from unnatural excitement; and they selected for this purpose a word (neepho), the acknowledged meaning of which at that time, was total abstinence from wine, or such a sober state of body and mind as is consequent on this abstinence. This is the very word used in Greek to express the abstinence enjoined upon the priests during their ministrations; and, whether the apostles intended to convey the full sense of the term or not, its very selection intimated their conviction that the sobriety which was based on total abstinence was that which they could most cordially approve. To break the force of this conclusion, attention is often drawn to the passages in which bishops are enjoined 'not to be given to wine,' and deacons and elder women 'not to be given to much wine:' hence it is inferred that some wine was permitted. But (1) cautions against excess can never be held to express approval of the acts referred to. 'Let not the sun go down upon your wrath' is not an approval of wrath while the sun is above the horizon. (2) A general condemnation of all that was comprised under the name of wines (Greek oinoi, Latin vina), would have included some drinks perfectly harmless. (3) Bishops were to be 'not given to wine' (literally, 'not near to wine'), and both these and deacons wives were enjoined to be 'abstinent' (nephalious), a command not to be obeyed by any indulgence in wines capable of exciting the animal nature and deadening the mental and spiritual powers. It may, in conclusion, be affirmed that the New Testament does not contradict, but coincides with, the letter of the Old, while the ideal of religious perfection it holds up to imitation calls for the exercise of the greatest self-restraint in leading to separation from articles whose influence for evil, on the bodies and minds of men, has been universally lamented. The 'moderation' alluded to in Phil. iv. 5 is not moderation in wine-drinking or any kind of drinking, but moderation of mind in the midst of injustice and suffering from without."

Vine gives nepho as a Greek word for our English verb watch, and says it means "to abstain from wine, is used metaphorically of moral alterness, and translated to watch, in the A.V. of 2 Tim. 4:5."

In the foregoing I have established that abstinence from wine, and avoiding proximity to wine are enjoined upon Christians by the Apostle Paul — nephaleon, to abstain from wine and me paroinon, not near wine. We have two more Greek expressions that must be considered.

1 Tim. 3:8, "Likewise must the deacons be grave, not doubletongued, not given to much wine" (me oino pollo prosechontas — not wine much addicted to). Prosechontas comes from prosecho which Vine says in this verse is used of giving oneself up to. Verse 11, "Even so must their wives be sober (nephaleous" — abstain from wine).

Titus 2:2,3, "That the aged men (presbutas — elders) be sober (nephalious — abstain from wine), grave, temperate (sophronas — self controlled, soberminded, self restrained — see Vine), sound in faith, in charity, in patience. The aged women (presbutidas) likewise, that they be in behaviour as becometh holiness, not false accusers, not given to much wine" (me oino pollo dedoulomenas — not wine much enslaved).

Two different words are used in the above passages, but they convey the same meaning and there is no objection to the way the translators have rendered them. Prosechontas comes from prosecho which here has the sense of giving oneself up to. Dedoulomenas means enslaved to, wholly given up to. (See vine, Thayer, and others.)

The words "not given to much wine" must be studied in connection with the immediate contexts and also with other Scriptures dealing with wine. If we assume that there is an implied consent to some wine in this expression, we get ourselves into a ridiculous situation.

It is definite that nephaleon (nephalious, nephaleous) means to abstain from wine, and me paroinon means not to be near wine. Now, let us assume that there is an implied consent to drinking moderately in this expression, that "not given to much wine" means to use wine moderately. This brings us to the absolute ridiculous.

1 Tim. 3:2,3 tells us that bishops must abstain from wine (nephaleon), and not even be near wine (me paroinon). Verse 8 permits deacons to drink wine (me oino pollo prosechontas). Verse 11 requires deacons wives to abstain from wine (nephaleous). Titus 1:7 requires bishops to not come near wine (me paroinon). Titus 2:2 requires aged men to not come near wine (me paroinon). Titus 2:3 permits aged women to drink wine.

And so we have a "reductio ad absurdum," but this is where the implied consent takes us. If you are a bishop you must abstain. If you are a deacon, you may drink. If you are a deacon's wife, you must abstain. If you are an aged man, you must abstain. If you are an aged woman, you may drink. Now what is the woman to do who is both aged and a deacon's wife? Perhaps she could alternate, be a deacon's wife one day and abstain and an aged woman the next day and drink.

Me par oinon — not near wine has its counterpart in Prov. 23:31, "Look not thou upon the wine when it is red, when it giveth his colour in the cup, when it moveth itself aright." The entire passage from verse 29 to verse 35 shows that fermented wine is indicated. The writer of Proverbs says, "Don't look upon it." The Apostle says, "Don't go near it." The Prophet Habakkuk says it is poison — "Woe unto him that giveth his neighbour drink, that puttest thy bottle (Hebrew — khamah, poison) to him" (Hab. 2:15).

I have shown in the foregoing pages that the use of fermented wine is condemned in the Scriptures, but the implied consent advocates ignore them and build their case for moderation on assumed implied meaning of these two passages, an assumption that contradicts all the divine pronouncements and denunciations against wine that "moveth itself aright" (that is fermented). This is a violation of the rules of Biblical interpretation mentioned in the first part of this chapter.

By assuming their implied consent position is true, and then following it to its logical conclusion, we have seen how ridiculous it becomes.

God knew, even before Noah got tipsy, that fermented wine contains a poison we call alcohol (C_2H_5OH), and He had His prophet warn us that we give our neighbour poison (khamah) when we give him this kind of wine. God has ever known the poisonous, habit-forming, addiction-producing effects caused by this drug known as alcohol. Modern science confirms what has been in the Bible for three thousand years. Dr. Andrew C. Ivy gave us this definition of alcohol at The Institute of Scientific Studies on Alcoholism, held at the College of Medical Evangelists (now Loma Linda University in Calif.), in 1952, and also at our National Temperance League Training School at Illinois Wesleyan University:

"Alcohol, from a pharmacological and medical viewpoint, is an intoxicating, hypnotic, analgesic, anesthetic, poisonous, and potentially habit-forming, craving-producing or addiction-producing drug." Dr. Ivy was Vice-President of Illinois University, and head of the University's Medical College in Chicago, and the most informed man on the problems of alcoholism that this writer has ever known.

The Lord, knowing more than all the scientists put together about the nature of alcohol and the problems it creates, instructed His Apostles and Prophets to admonish us to abstain from drinking it, not to look upon it, not to go near it, lest we become addicted to it.

The liquor industry admits the dangers of addiction to those who drink. The Licensed Beverage Industries, in their Facts Book for 1968, make this statement on page 11, "The overwhelming majority of drinkers in the U.S. — an estimated 90 per cent of them — have apparently learned to consume alcoholic beverages without significant hazard to themselves, their families, or society."

This is an adverse admission on the part of the Licensed Beverage Industries that the consumption of alcoholic beverages does become a significant hazard to the drinker himself, or his family, or society, on the scale of one out of every ten persons who drink. The liquor industry now admits what temperance speakers were stating more than forty years ago. But this statement was made for the purpose of minimizing the harm caused by drink, and also for the purpose of justifying their traffic. Only one out of ten persons who drink experiences significant hazard to himself, his family, or society! Only one out of ten drinkers brings shame, suffering, sorrow to himself, his family, or society! The consumption of alcoholic beverages has become a significant hazard to his family, or society, or himself — to only 9,000,000 Americans! How insensitive have we become! We would cry with the Prophet Jeremiah, "Is it nothing to you, all ye that pass by?" (Lam. 1:12).

Even nine million is an understatement. On June 9, 1979 the Detroit News carried a report on an address that Dr. George W. Gallup gave at the 191st General Assembly of the United Presbyterian Church on the survey the Gallup Poll had just made on drinking in the United States. The Gallup survey revealed that 23 per cent of the people of America admit to "overindulgence on occasion," and he also stated, "Today, one person in four (25 per cent) says that an alcohol-related problem has adversely affected his or her family life." The Census Bureau reported that on January 1, 1979 the population of the United States had reached 219,500,000. Then, according to the Gallup Poll's finding of 25 percent, 54,872,500 Americans have had adversity, misfortune, trouble, sorrow brought into their homes by drink.

Recently a booklet, "Prepared and distributed in the community interest by Blue Cross Blue Shield of Michigan" called "The Alcoholic American," was given to me. I quote this jolting statement from this booklet: "Potential for Alcoholism. Everyone is human and more than 75 percent of adult Americans at one time or another drink alcoholic beverages, so alcoholism is a potential hazard to almost everyone. Dr. William B. Terhune, in The Safeway to Drink, says, 'Man has enjoyed alcohol's pleasant effects for a long time and lived by the myth that he will not become addicted. But let's explode this myth right now. In the course of a lifetime, one out of eight adults now living in the United States will become either alcoholic or seriously handicapped by alcohol dependency. Everyone is vulnerable.'"

A fact that must be emphasized here is that every alcoholic and alcohol dependent who has become enslaved by much wine, "given to much wine," never intended to become so. The alcoholic was first an occasional or moderate drinker before he became an alcoholic, addicted to, enslaved by, "given to much wine." The road to alcoholism starts with the first drink. No one ever becomes an alcoholic who is and continues to be an abstainer. And the only cure for alcoholism is for the alcoholic to become a total abstainer. He dare not try to return to moderate drinking. Moderation will be the cause of his downfall again. This is a fact that the alcoholic must understand, and that every counsellor who endeavors to help an alcoholic must emphasize.

Another fact that should be impressed upon every drinker and non-drinker is that there is not a scientist, psychiatrist, psychologist, physiologist, theologist, or bartender who can line up eight or ten persons and pick out the one who will become an alcoholic or alcohol dependent, if he begins to drink, and can guarantee that the rest in the lineup can drink without any danger of becoming an alcoholic.

The only way that any person can be certain that he or she will not become addicted, or that his or her drinking will never "become a significant hazard to himself, his family, or society" is to be nephaleon (abstain from wine), me paroinon (not go near wine). This is the only guarantee to be me oino pollo prosechontas (not enslaved by much wine).

I have shown that the true meaning of the Greek words that Paul uses in the requirements enjoined upon bishops is that he abstain from wine (nephaleon), and not go near wine (me paroinon). If implied consent to drink wine moderately is given in me oino pollo prosechontas (not given to much wine) and deacons are permitted to have wine in the house and drink it, how can the bishop visit the home of the deacon, who has his own bottle on the table, without violating me paroinon which forbids the bishop to be near wine. Carrying the implied consent interpretation a bit further, what must be going through the mind of the aged man who is forbidden to drink (nephalious), as he sits across the table from his wife who is enjoying her glass of wine? Of course the situation is reversed for the deacon and his wife. She stares across the table at him with his glass of wine in his hand while she has to abstain (nephaleous).

Can the God who, in Proverbs, warned us not to look upon fermented wine, who, in Habakkuk, pronounced woe upon him who gives his neighbour poison, who, in 1 Timothy and Titus, commanded bishops to abstain and not go near wine, and required aged men and deacon's wives to abstain, can He be so capricious as to tell deacons and aged women, at least by implication, that they may imbibe, if they do so moderately?

In stating the qualifications for bishops, elders, deacons, and their wives, Paul is dealing with spiritual standards, moral values, ethics, Christian virtues. With exception of certain requirements for those in positions of leadership, God, because of His own nature, righteousness, and holiness can set only one standard of morality, righteousness and holiness which all are to follow and "without which no man shall see the Lord" (Heb. 12:14).

Because of the blight and wreck and ruin that is caused by alcohol, the manufacture, distribution, sale, and consumption of intoxicating beverages is a moral issue.

On moral issues, righteousness, and holiness, the standard must be for all, whether apostles, prophets, bishops, elders, pastors, deacons, humble "doorkeepers in the house of my Lord," or their wives.

In 1 Tim. 3:1-7 we find seventeen requirements that a man must meet if he "desire the office of a bishop." In verses 8-13 we have ten requirements listed for deacons. Does this mean that God sets one standard for bishops and a different standard for deacons? Being "not doubletongued" is not listed in the requirements for bishops, but it is listed for deacons. Does this mean that a bishop is permitted to be doubletongued? Both are required to be "the husband of one wife," but it is specified what kind of wife the deacon must have and says nothing about what kind a bishop should have, except that he have only one. Are we to understand by this that bishop's wives are not required to be "grave, not slanderers, sober (nephalious—abstain from wine), faithful in all things?"

In 1 Tim. 3 and Titus 1 & 2, where we find requirements of bishops, deacons, deacon's wives, aged men (elders), and aged women, I cannot find any requirements regarding righteousness, holiness and general conduct

154

applied to one group that should not apply to all, and I believe the moderationists would agree with me here, except being abstinent from wine. No Christian, regardless of his or her position in the Church, and no non-Christian for that matter, should be enslaved by wine (me oino pollo prosechontas). To avoid wine enslavement, all Christians, and non-Christians, should be nephaleous (abstain from wine) and me paroinon (not go near wine). This is in harmony with the whole tenor of Biblical teaching on wine. The implied consent to moderation theory is contrary to Biblical teaching.

The Bible gives the Christian two laws regarding wine. First is the law of abstinence from fermented wine. Second is the law of Christian example.

Paul wrote Timothy, "Let no man despise thy youth; but be thou an example of the believers, in word, in conversation, in charity, in spirit, in purity" (1 Tim. 4:12). The law of Christian example requires us to so conduct ourselves that others may see in us a true pattern of the Christian life. Our conduct, how we live, what we do, bears an influence on others.

As Christians we are to so walk that others may follow our footsteps and not go astray. We are to so live that others may safely life likewise, and the word likewise is the word used in the passages we have been studying. This is brought out in Titus 2:2,3. Regarding wine, Paul writes, "That the aged men be sober" (nephalious — abstain from wine). For their wives, the aged women, Paul writes that they should be me oino pollo dedoulomenas (not given to much wine). But if they are not to be given to much wine, how are they to be in regard to wine? The third verse opens with, "The aged women likewise" (housautos — meaning — in like manner, just so, Vine & Thayer). Likewise, in like manner, refers to what has preceded. In like manner to the aged men. The aged men are to be nephalious. In like manner, likewise are the aged women to be (nephaleous, abstain from wine), and so being they will me oino pollo dedoulomenas (not be enslaved by much wine).

Those in higher positions of leadership and authority are to so conduct themselves that those under them can emulate their lives. So bishops are to abstain from wine and not go near it, and Paul says deacons are to be me oino pollo prosechontas (not addicted to wine). How are they to avoid addiction? By emulating the bishops. Likewise (housautos — in like manner), as the bishops they should be nephaleon. As the bishops are, "Likewise the deacons must be . . ."

Proof that I am not straining a point here is in 1 Tim. 3:11, where Paul writes about the deacons wives, immediately following the requirements of deacons, "Even so (hosautos — in like manner, likewise) must their wives be grave, not slanderers, sober" (nephaleous — abstain from wine). How could their wives be nephaleous in like manner as their husbands if their husbands were not nephaleous? There is no other purpose for use of the word hosautos (likewise).

In Rom. 14 Paul deals with eating meat that has been offered to idols, whether or not Christians should eat such meats. In verse 21 he sets forth a principle for Christians to follow. This is the law of Christian example. "It is good neither to eat flesh, nor to drink wine, nor any thing whereby thy brother stumbleth, or is offended, or is made weak."

155

If my walk is such that those who follow my footsteps may stumble, or be offended, or be made weak, I am violating the law of Christian example. The adverse admission of the Licensed Beverage Industries is that one out of every ten who drink will stumble, be offended, or made weak. The Blue Cross Blue Shield of Michigan quotes Dr. Terhune's statement that, "In the course of a lifetime, one out of eight adults now living in the United States will become either alcoholic or seriously handicapped by alcohol dependency. Everyone is vulnerable." The Gallup Poll shows that more than 54 million Americans have been offended by an alcohol-related problem in their family. On June 11, 1975, in a conversation I had with Dr. Andrew C. Ivy, he stated that America had, at that time, 9 million alcoholics and 16 million or more alcohol-dependent, or pre-alcoholics, a total of 25 million Americans who have stumbled and been made weak by drink.

My life and conduct is considered by others as an example of what a Christian should do and be. If somehow I could be given assurance that I would never become alcoholic, or bring any harm to myself, my family, or society by drinking, because of the influence my drinking might have on others, the law of Christian example in Rom. 14:21 requires me to abstain from wine (nephaleon). If Ewing can drink, he's a Christian and a preacher, why shouldn't I? This is the message my drinking, even though it be moderate, would send out to others, and one out of every ten, according to L.B.I., who follow my example would stumble, be offended, be made weak.

The law of Christian example requires me to set a right example so that those who emulate me will not stumble. Dr. Ivy's simple definition of right and wrong is, "That which injures ourself or someone else is wrong. That which helps ourself or someone else or does not injure ourself or someone else is right." Paul writes, "The right course (or thing) is not to eat meat, nor to drink wine, nor to do anything through which your brother is made to stumble" (See translations by Weymouth, Moffatt, Williams, Rev. Stan. Ver., Centenary Trans., Schonfield, Today's Eng. Ver., Twentieth Cent. Ver., Ampl. N.T.). God's Word requires me to do right, and to abstain from wrong.

In view of all the Scriptures that admonish us to abstain from and avoid fermented wine and strong drink (shekar), I can find no implied consent to drink moderately in the expression "not given to much wine." Implied consent is contrary to the general admonition of all the other Scriptures. Would the Holy Spirit move Paul to tell the Corinthians not to drink wine because of its being a stumbling block to others, and then move him in writing to Timothy and Titus to give sanction to drink wine.

John Wesley, founder of the Methodist Church, said in 1744, "You see the wine when it sparkles in the cup, and are going to drink it. I say, there is poison in it, and therefore, beg you to throw it away. If you add, 'It is not poison to me, though it may be to others;' then I say, 'throw it away for thy brother's sake, lest thou embolden him to drink also. Why should thy strength occasion thy weak brother to perish, for whom Christ died?'" (From Cyclopedia of Temperance and Prohibition).

This then is the message: as an example to others, and to be me oino pollo prosechontas (not enslaved by much wine, not become an alcoholic), we are to abstain from wine (nephaleon) and not even go near it, not have it around (me paroinon), nor do "any thing whereby thy brother stumbleth, or is offended, or is made weak." Untold millions have stumbled by believing there is no harm in moderation, but their moderation led to enslavement, and those who sanctioned moderation, by word or example, share in the responsibility for their downfall.

Chapter 45

CONCLUSION

In this treatise, I have presented evidence to prove that the word wine as used in the Bible does not always mean a fermented, intoxicating drink. Neither do the Hebrew and Greek words that it translates. We have been dealing with generic terms, words that have multiple meanings. One of these meanings is the sweet unfermented juice of the grape. Another meaning is the fermented grape juice.

It is a mistake to assume that whenever these Hebrew or Greek words are used in the original texts, or whenever the English word wine is used in translating them, fermented wine is always and only indicated. To assume this make the Bible full of self-contradictions, and robs it of its divine authority, for God cannot contradict Himself. I have given numerous instances where the word wine cannot possibly mean that which is fermented. Fermented wine does not hang on the vine. Men do not tread out fermented wine. Fermented wine is not "the fruit of the vine."

I have given texts which show that God's approval, sanctions, and blessings are given to wine. I have given other texts where His disapproval, condemnation, prohibitions are given to wine. How can this be if wine is always fermented and intoxicating? God cannot bless what He has condemned and He cannot condemn what He has blessed. He who not only condemns adultery, but also condemns looking upon a woman to lust after her, cannot condemn drunkenness and then bless that which causes the drunkenness.

I have shown in this study that wine is used to translate words that mean both fermented and unfermented grape juice. How are we to know which kind of wine is indicated by a specific verse? In many instances the way the word is used in thes entence will indicate whether it refers to the grape in the cluster on the vine, the freshly expressed juice of the grape, the juice preserved from fermentation by cooking or some other method, the grapes in the form of dried raisins, or the fermented and intoxicating grape juice. The reader can also consult a good concordance, say Strong's or Young's, and find the Hebrew or Greek word in any text, and then by referring to the definitions I have given in this treatise learn the intended meaning of any verse of Scripture dealing with our subject.

Whenever God's blessing, sanction, approval is given to the fruit of the vine, it can only indicate that which is nonintoxicating, unfermented. Whenever condemnation, warning, prohibitions are attached to wine, or palm sap, it denotes that which is fermented and intoxicating.

"Who hath woe? who hath sorrow? who hath contentions? who hath babbling? who hath wounds without cause? who hath redness of eyes? They

159

that tarry long at the wine; they that go to seek mixed wine. Look not thou upon the wine when (at the time that, at which time, during which time) it is red, when (at the time that) it giveth his colour in the cup, when (at the time that) it moveth itself aright. At the last it biteth like a serpent, and stingeth like an adder. Thine eyes shall behold strange women, and thine heart shall utter perverse things. Yea, thou shalt be as he that lieth down in the midst of the sea, or as he that lieth upon the top of a mast. They have stricken me, shalt thou say, and I was not sick; they beaten me, and I felt it not: when shall I awake: I will seek it yet again" (Prov. 23:29-35). Now does the sweet, unfermented, nonalcoholic wine cause what is pictured here, or is it caused by the fermented, intoxicating, alcoholic wine?

"Wine is a mocker, strong drink is raging: and whosoever is deceived thereby is not wise" (Prov. 20:1). Sweet unfermented wine is no mocker. It is not raging. It does not deceive the user. Fermented wine is the mocker, rager, deceiver.

In these two passages as well as numerous others in the Bible, the verse itself indicates the meaning of the word wine.

The pure juice of the grape, unfermented wine, and palm sap, are among those blessings that God has given to man for his enjoyment, benefit and health. God sanctions their use.

Fermented wine is the product of corruption, and it has been a corruptor of mankind throughout the ages.

"Look not thou upon the wine when it is fermented" (Prov. 23:31, literal meaning).

BIBLIOGRAPHY

American Peoples Encyclopedia, Spencer Press, Chicago, 1953.

American Standard Version of the Holy Bible, John A. Dickson Publishing Co., 1901.

Amplified Bible, Zondervan Publishing, House, Grand Rapids, Michigan.

Bailey, Nathan, The New Universal English Dictionary of Words and of Arts and Sciences, Carefully Corrected by Mr. Buchanan, Printed for James Rivington and James Fletcher in Pater-noster-row, 4th Edition, 1759.

Ben-Yehuda, Ehud, Ben-Yehuda's Pocket English-Hebrew, Hebrew-English Dictionary, Washington Square Press, Inc., New York, 1964.

Berkeley Version of the Holy Bible, Zondervan Publishing House, Grand Rapids, 1959.

Bullinger, E.W., D.D., The Companion Bible, Oxford University Press, London, New York, Toronto, Melbourne.

Burns, Dawson, M.A., F.S.S., The Bases of the Temperance Reform; an Exposition and Appeal, National Temperance Society and Publication House, New York, 1873.

Collier's Encyclopedia, Article-Wine Palm, Caxton Publishing Co., Toronto, 1960.

Concordant Version, The Sacred Scriptures, With a Uniform Sublinear Word for Word Translation and a Consistent Emphasized English Version, The Concordant Publishing Concern, Los Angeles, 1930.

Crawley, A.E., Article in Encyclopedia of Religion and Ethics, Edited by James Hastings, Charles Scribner & Sons, New York, 1951.

Cyclopedia of Temperance and Prohibition, Funk & Wagnalls, New York, 1891.

Davidson, Benjamin, Analytical Hebrew and Chaldee Lexicon, Samuel Bagster and Sons, Ltd., London, Harper and Brothers, New York.

Davies, Benjamin, Ph.D., LL.D., A Compendious and Complete Hebrew and Chaldee Lexicon, New Edition Revised by Edward C. Mitchell, D.D., Bradley & Woodruff, 1875.

Davis, John B., Ph.D., D.D., LL.D., A Dictionary of the Bible, The Westminster Press, Philadelphia, 1920.

Dobyns, Fletcher, The Amazing Story of Repeal, Willett, Clark & Company, Chicago, New York, 1940.

Douglas, George C.M., D.D., Fairbairn's Imperial Standard Bible Encyclopedia, Edited by Patrick Fairnbairn, D.D., Zondervan Publishing House, Grand Rapids, 1957.

Edersheim, Alfred, M.A. (Oxon), D.D., Ph.D., The Life and Times of Jesus the Messiah, New American Edition, E.R. Herrick & Company, New York.

Encyclopedia Americana, Americana Corporation, New York, 1957 Edition, 1965 Edition.

Encyclopedia Britannica, Encyclopedia Britannica, Inc., New York, 8th Edition 1853, 14th Edition 1929, 1958, 1964.

Englishman's Greek New Testament, The, Zondervan Publishing House, Grand Rapids, 1970.

English Revised Version, The Holy Bible, Oxford University Press, London, 1885.

Fenton, Ferrar, M.R.A.S., M.C.A.A., Etc. The Bible and Wine, A. & C. Black, Ltd., London.

Fenton, Ferrar, M.R.A.S., M.C.A.A., The Holy Bible in Modern English, Destiny Publishers, Merrimac, Mass.

Funk & Wagnalls College Standard Dictionary, Condensed from Funk & Wagnalls New Standard Dictionary 1922 Edition, Funk & Wagnalls Company, New York, 1936.

Funk & Wagnalls Desk Standard Dictionary, Funk & Wagnalls Company, New York, 1946.

Funk & Wagnalls Standard College Dictionary, Third Edition, contained in The Reader's Digest Great Encyclopedic Dictionary, The Reader's Digest Association, Inc., Pleasantville, New York, 1969.

Funk & Wagnalls Standard Family Dictionary, Funk & Wagnalls Company, Standard Reference Works Publishing Company, Inc., New York, 1961.

Gordon, Ernest, Christ, The Apostles and Wine, The Sunday School Times, Philadelphia, 1944.

Hastings, James, Encyclopedia of Religion and Ethics, Charles Scribner & Sons, New York, 1951.

Haggard, Howard W., and Jellineck, E.M., Alcohol Explored, Doubleday, Doran & Company, Inc., Garden City, New York, 1945.

Herodotus, The History of, Translated by George Rawlinson, Edited by Manuel Komroff, Dial Press, Inc., Tudor Publishing Company, New York, 1928.

Hitt, Fred G., The Truth About Wine, March 1936 issue of The Kingdom Digest, Dallas.

Host's Handbook, The, Fourth Edition, National Distillers Products Corporation, New York, 1940.

Hughes, Mary, Article-The Land Is Mine, Sept. 1970 issue of The Kingdom Digest, Dallas.

Ivy, Andrew C., Ph.D., M.D., D.Sc., LL.D., Definition of Terms Basic to the Problems Created by the Consumption of Alcohol, Lecture given at Third Session, Institute of Scientific Studies for the Prevention of Alcoholism, Loma Linda, Calif., 1952.

Jewish Encyclopedia, The, Ktav Publishing House, Inc., New York, 1943.

Josephus, Flavius, The Life and Works of, Translated by William Whiston, A.M., The John Winston Company, Philadelphia, Toronto, 1957.

Lamsa, George M., The Holy Bible Translated from Eastern Manuscripts, Containing the Old and New Testaments Translated from the Peshitta, A.J. Holman Company, Philadelphia, 1957.

Lees, F.R., Cyclopedia of Temperance and Prohibition, Funk & Wagnalls, New York, 1891.

Lees, F.R., Text Book of Temperance, Rockwell & Robbins, 1869.

Leeser, Isaac, The Holy Bible (Old Testament), Translation Revised, Hebrew Publishing Company, New York, 1926.

Lund, Roy S., Should Churches Use Wine for Communion?, Published by Roy S. Lund, Valley City, North Dakota.

McClintock and Strong, Cyclopedia of Biblical, Theological and Ecclesiastical Literature, Harper & Brothers, Franklin Square, New York, 1881.

Moffatt, James D., D.D., D.Litt., M.A. (Oxon), The Holy Bible, A New Translation, Doubleday, Doran & Company, Inc., Garden City, New York, 1926.

Montgomery, Helen Barrett, A.M., D.H.L., LL.D., Centenary Translation, The New Testament in Modern English, American Baptist Publication Society, The Judson Press, Philadelphia, Chicago, etc., 1924.

National Geographic, National Geographic Society, Washington, April 1966, Oct. 1970, Mar. 1971.

New American Encyclopedic Dictionary, The, Five Volumes, J.A. Hill & Company, New York, 1906.

Now Catholic Edition of the Holy Bible Translated from the Latin Vulgate, The Old Testament Douay Version, The New Testament Confraternity Edition a revision of the Challoner-Rheims Version, Catholic Book Publishing Company, New York, 1951.

New Century Dictionary, The, The Century Company, New York, 1927.

New English Bible New Testament, Oxford University Press, Cambridge University Press, London, 1961.

New World Translation of the Holy Scriptures, Rendered from the Original Languages by the New World Translation Committee, O.T. Copyright 1953-1960, by Watch Tower Bible & Tract Society of Penna., N.T. Copyright 1950 by Watch Tower Bible & Tract Society, Published by Watch Tower Bible & Tract Society, Inc., International Bible Students Association, Brooklyn.

Oxford English Dictionary, Oxford Universal Press, London, 1933.

Panin, Ivan, Numerio English New Testament, The N.T. From the Greek Text as Established by Bible Numerics, The Book Society of Canada, Toronto, 1954.

Patton, William, Bible Wines or Laws of Fermentation and Wines of the Ancients, 1871, republished by Sane Press, Sooner Alcohol-Narcotics Education, 101 N.E. 23rd St., Oklahoma City, 1974.

Phillips, J.B., The New Testament in Modern English, Christianity Today Inc. Edition, Produced by The Iverson-Ford Associates, New York, 1967.

Pixley, Victor A., Documentary Evidence that the Wine at the Lords' Supper Was Unfermented, Published by Victor A. Pixley, Long Island City, N.Y. 1958.

Pixley, Victor A., Review & Comments on Dr. Brown's Lutheran Article "Wine or Grape Juice?", Published by Victor A. Pixley, Long Island City, N.Y. 1960.

Popular and Critical Bible Encyclopedia and Scriptural Dictionary, Edited by Samuel Fallows, A.M., D.D., LL.D., Andrew C. Zenos, A.M., D.D., and Herbert L. Willett, A.M., Ph.D., The Howard Severance Company, Chicago, 1904.

Random House Dictionary of the English Language, Unabridged Edition, Random House, New York, 1966.

Revised Standard Version, The Holy Bible, Thomas Nelson & Sons, New York, 1952.

Rimmer, Harry, D.D., Sc.D., Article-What About Wine "For Stomach's Sake," in The National Voice, also The Voice of Temperance Scrap Book Number Two, Sam Morris, Bunker Printing and Lithographing Co., Fort Worth, Texas, 1940.

Rotherham, Joseph Bryant, The Emphasized Bible, Kregel Publications, Grand Rapids, 1959.

Rubin, Dr. I.M., The Holy Bible, (Old Testament), Star Hebrew Book Co., New York, 1928.

Samson, G.W., Cyclopedia of Temperance and Prohibition, Funk & Wagnalls, New York, 1891.

Schirmacher, Stan, Wine' It's In The Bible, Osterhus Publishing House, Minneapolis.

Septuagint Version of the Old Testament, The, With an English Translation by Sir Launcelot Lee Brenton, Samuel Bagster and Sons, Ltd. London, Harper and Brothers, New York.

Shedd, James, Dictionaries and That Dictionary, Scott, Foreman and Company, Chicago, 1962.

Smith, J.M. Powis, Goodspeed, Edgar J., Smith Goodspeed Bible, The Bible An American Translation, University of Chicago Press, Chicago, 1935.

Smith, William, LL.D., A Dictionary of the Bible, Revised and Edited by Rev. V.N. and M.A. Peloubet, Zondervan Publishing House, Grand Rapids, 1967.

Strong, James, S.T.D., LL.D., Exhaustive Concordance of the Bible, Abingdon-Cokesbury Press, New York, Eighteenth Printing 1948.

Thayer, Joseph Henry, D.D., A Greek-English Lexicon of the New testament, Corrected Edition, American Book Company, New York, Cincinnati, Chicago, 1889.

Twentieth Century New Testament, The, A Translation into Modern English, Moody Press, Chicago.

Universal Jewish Encyclopeida, The Universal Jewish Encyclopedia, Inc. New York, 1943.

Wagner, Philip M., American Wines and Wine Making, Alfred A. Knopf, New York, 1963.

Vermont Maple Sugar and Syrup, Vermont Department of Agriculture, Montpelier, 1952.

Walker, William H. Does the Bible Teach Total Abstinence?, Prohibition National Committee, Denver.

Webster's Collegiate Dictionary, Third edition of the Merriam Series, G. & C. Merriam, Springfield, Mass., 1924.

Webster's Collegiate Dictionary Fifth Edition, G. & C. Merriam, Springfield, Mass., 1945.

Webster's Seventh New Collegiate Dictionary, G. & C. Merriam Company, Springfield, Mass. 1967.

Webster's New International Dictionary, Second Edition, G. & C. Merriam, Springfield, Mass. 1958.

Webster's Third International Dictionary, G. & C. Merriam Company, Springfield, Mass. 1959.

Williams, Charles B., The New Testament, A Private Translation in the Language of the People, Moody Press, Chicago, 1958.

Wilson, Benjamin, The Emphatic Diaglott, Containing the Original Greek Text of What Is Commonly Styled the New Testament, With An Interlineary Word for Word English Translation, and a New Emphatic Version Based on the Interlineary Translation. International Bible Students Association, Watch Tower Bible and Tract Society, Brooklyn, 1942.

World Book Encyclopedia, Field Enterprizes, Chicago, 1952, 1964.

Young, Robert, LL.D., Analytical Concordance of the Bible, Twentieth Century American Edition, Tenth Printing, Funk & Wagnalls Company, New York.

Young, Robert, LL.D., Young's Literal Translation of the Bible, Revised Edition, G.A. Young & Company, Bible Publishers, Edenburgh, Scotland, 1900.